SPEAK
INSPIRE
EMPOWER

How To Give Persuasive Presentations To Boost Your Confidence And Career

Mark Robinson

Copyright

Mark Robinson

Title: *"Speak Inspire Empower. How To Give Persuasive Presentations To Boost Your Confidence And Career"*
© 2020, Mark Robinson
Self-published

Contact: mark@markrobinsontraining.com

For purchasing in large quantities or for a special edition version with a custom cover (of either this book or the accompanying Presentation Planner), please contact the author.

Illustrator: Hani Javan Hemmat
                (Gilmard.com)
Editor: Simone Roach
                (linkedin.com/in/simone-roach-editor)

Disclaimer

I was a TEDx speaker for TEDxEindhoven in 2016. The following year I was a member of the curation team (the team responsible for everything that happens on stage). As part of this I was also a TEDx speaker coach, which I remain up to today (in 2020).

Apart from that, I'm not affiliated in any way with TED Conferences LLC and do not represent the opinions or policies of TED.

Praise for:
Speak Inspire Empower

Mark's book reads like a TED talk and builds your confidence as he takes you step by step through this journey of becoming an effective presenter. His experience and humility keep it real and relatable.
Johnna Stein – Training Director

It is stunning to realise while reading how poor our presentations are today and how many human hours per day are wasted listening to bad presentations. Mark shows in the book how easy and surprisingly simple the solutions are to making a presentation that really can have an impact.
Henk Niesing, Director Product Management

This book reveals some hard truths about what is wrong with many corporate presentations and goes on to address them with warmth, originality and depth. Speak Inspire Empower *is a breath of fresh air amongst the usual offering of "presentation skills best practice" books.*
Janice Haywood – Presentation Skills Trainer

A captivating read, with thought provoking illustrations and lots and lots of humour.
Lilly Rosier - Business Analyst

The core of TMC is to inspire engineers to become successful "Employeneurs". Some of them also become successful entrepreneurs. Mark is a living example of this idea: by setting up the highly acclaimed Mark Robinson Training, he is empowering his fellow engineers, and hundreds of others, to communicate confidently, persuasively and clearly! Everyone who wants to give great presentations and grow in self-confidence should follow his workshop and read this book!

Thijs Manders - Founder & President TMC Group, Founder & CEO TMI-Investments.com

The least likely TEDx-er

"Life begins at the end of your comfort zone."
Neale Donald Walsch - author

Waiting nervously to go on the TEDx stage, I reflected how crazy this would have seemed to me earlier in my life, even just a few months before.

I'm not a natural speaker. I can still find giving presentations scary, even to small groups.

Yet here I was, about to speak to 300 people (and later, hundreds of thousands) at TEDxEindhoven on the topic: *"How to present to keep your audience's attention"*

Over many years, I had developed *limiting beliefs* which said I couldn't speak in public, that I was not a presenter and that these kinds of opportunities only happened to other people.

And yet, one by one, I've defied these limiting beliefs, these *lies*. The goal of this book is that you will defy your limiting beliefs, starting with the one that may be the reason

1

you've bought this book: the false belief that, *"you can't speak well in front of a group."*

The truth is, **you can give a *great* presentation**. There are a few easy techniques you can apply to get and keep your audience's attention. You will learn and apply these along with many other techniques to persuade your audience and inspire them to action.

I wrote this book not only to instruct you but also to engage and inspire you. Or, as we will soon see, not only to Educate but also to Entertain and Empower.

This is not the story of a great public speaker. This is the story of an ordinary guy who learnt many techniques from a variety of sources which I then developed over years of practice.

This is my story. And if you apply the lessons in this book, an experience like this can become your story too.

But it all started with fear, on a day when I was absolutely terrified...

Contents

The least likely TEDx-er   1

Contents   3

Why develop your presentation skills?   10

    Confidence   10

    Career   11

    Charisma   11

    Why should you read *this* book?   13

    How to get the most from this book   14

Terrified   19

    What is a limiting belief?   23

The 3Es: why are most presentations so boring and how can you make a great presentation?   25

    Prepare for your reprogramming   25

    The Teacher   27

    The Jester   30

    The Superhero   32

    So why are so many presentations so mind-numbingly boring?   34

The day it all changed   38

The goal of your presentation (or why should I give you an hour of my life I will never get back?)   41

Not a goal   43

What is a presentation goal?   43

What should they remember?   44

How should they feel?   45

What should they do?   48

Popeye moment   53

How to prepare   56

Mind map   57

Kill your darlings   59

Use your lifeline: ask the audience   62

Practice   66

An evening at TMC   72

How to start: get and keep their attention   77

How not to start   79

Part 1: three questions   84

Part 2: greeting + name + X minutes   87

Part 3: WII4ME   88

Part 4: a great way to continue   91

A presentation at ASML   94

A simple yet powerful structure that works for any
presentation   96

The French teacher   96

What is the Problem?   99

What is the Cause?   99

What are the Possible Solutions?   100

What is the Chosen or Recommended Solution?   101

How will your solution benefit your audience? 102

But I don't have a Problem! 103

Shorter version 104

Filling the auditorium and turning more away! 107

How to end: launch them into action! 111

3MP 112

C2A 113

TQ 117

Series of presentations 118

Pitching for TEDx 121

What should you do in the final second? 126

Why is the final second important? 126

How not to end your presentation 128

So, how should you end? 128

The four steps to unleash applause 130

Am I dreaming? 133

What was that about questions? 135

Why are questions so powerful? 135

Normal sentence? 136

How can I introduce the next topic? 137

Hands up those who think questions are an effective way to get attention? 139

Preparing for TEDx 144

Once upon a time... 147

Mystery 148

Ingredients 149

Timing 154

Keep them in suspense 155

Why are stories so powerful? 159

Speaking at TEDx! 166

Help! I'm nervous! Building self-confidence 173

Healthy fear 173

Practice 175

Not a monster 176

Power pose 176

Smile 180

Admit your nerves 181

Glass of water 182

And always remember... 183

The first workshops 186

The elephant in the room: PowerPoint 189

The Dangers of PowerPoint 190

Why do so many people use PowerPoint? 194

The Naked Presenter 196

No PowerPoint? Then what's the alternative? 197

Are there *any* circumstances when you *should* use PowerPoint? 198

Tips for using PowerPoint 203

Finally... 210

Mark Robinson Training 215

A man with a plan 215

First-ever full-day workshop 217

A treasure chest of extras 221

Presentation notes   222

What should I wear?   223

Give this presentation in an hour; here are the slides!   223

Remove dead phrases   225

Presentation title?   227

Intonation and slowing down: talk to 5-year-olds   228

Two-minute pitch   229

Presenting via video / online   233

The Flywheel   238

Learning from the best: advanced techniques in oratory and persuasion   241

POTUS 44: the sound of silence   242

POTUS 45: win, win, win!   245

POTUS 42-45   252

Nice   257

Influence, persuasion, hypnosis: casting a spell over your audience   260

The power of the direct command   260

My experience   264

The most subtle command   265

The John Lennon moment   266

With great power comes great responsibility   267

Becoming an author   271

Space, time and... body language?   275

Past & Future   275

Emphasis   278

What about my hands? 280

Drawing with your hands 282

The future 287

STAR moments 289

9 out of 10? Not good enough! 289

Ingredients 291

Join the audience 292

The star vandal 293

The Rick trick 294

Speak like TED to get ahead! 294

The long wait 297

Throwing away your notes 297

Ilka's paper 298

Lists of 3s 299

The SEX guy: acronyms and alliterations 300

Plastic bag 303

Drawings 304

A live vote 306

Bill Gates' TED talk 307

Maths professor 309

The life-changing power of positive feedback 313

My USP 313

Positive feedback in practice 315

Positive feedback on the first-ever workshop 316

Hannah 318

Daphne 322

The team   328

Me   330

Why it works   331

Life-changing   335

Don't believe me? Try it!   336

Life's walk of fame   338

Stand out   339

Be brave   340

Speak. Inspire. Empower.   341

Thanks   343

Appendix A: Obama's body language   347

Appendix B: Hani's journey: "making it simple is not simple"
                                                            351

Why develop your presentation skills?

"The best way I ever found to help overcome fear and develop courage and self-confidence rapidly is by speaking before groups."
Frank Bettger - salesman, author & speaker

Let's start with you. What is the reason you picked up this book? What do *you* hope to gain? If you were known as someone who can speak confidently and with authority in front of a group, how would that benefit you?

There are three ways in which your life will improve if you develop your presentation skills. Let's consider them one at a time.

Confidence

"Life shrinks or expands in proportion to one's courage."
Anais Nin - author

The better your presentation skills are, the more confident you will become! If you learn to speak confidently in front of a group, you will be more confident in speaking everywhere: either in a social setting like a party or on a date or in a business setting, for example, at a job interview. And becoming more confident means being more secure in who you are, and hence more authentic.

So develop your presentation skills onstage and you will confidently present your true self offstage. And because the world meets the real you: everyone wins!

But it gets better: if you are more confident, your presentations will also get better: you will also dare to be your authentic self in front of a group. You will be able to think more clearly on your feet and you will speak with more authority.

Career

Beyond that extra confidence, if you can communicate your message *at work* clearly, persuasively and in a way that people *want* to listen, then you will be seen as the expert on whatever topic on which you speak. People, including managers, will *want* to hear your presentations which will cause you to become a popular presenter.

And if you can get paid to give speeches, your income will increase dramatically!

Charisma

Great presentation skills are essential for leaders and anyone looking to inspire others. There are two reasons for this. The first is the *communication of your vision*. If you can make people enthusiastic about building a better tomorrow through your words, then you will **inspire** them.

And that brings me to the second reason: if they are inspired, they are more likely to follow your commands. Throughout this book, I will explain the need to take the lead when you are presenting to a group. Part of this involves giving *direct commands* to your audience. If you do this with *their* interests in mind, you will **empower** them.

How does this benefit you? When people get used to following your instructions, and as you get used to giving them, your ability to lead them will also develop. In short, you will develop your *charisma*.

Why should you read *this* book?

This is not a standard presentation skills book. If you're looking for a book that helps you create beautiful PowerPoint slides, there are many good books on those topics.

But if you are looking for an encouraging, fun and motivating book which above all else teaches you *practical techniques* to **speak**, **inspire** and **empower**, this is it!

This book is actually two books in one:

1. The main content of this book is based on my presentation skills workshop. This content has been refined through dozens of workshops to many hundreds of people. The average score from my workshops is 9.5 / 10. So you can be confident that you will learn quality lessons from this book. Whether your presentation skills right now are good, bad or ugly, or even if you are terrified of public speaking, as I was, this book will help you get to *TEDx* level.
2. Interwoven between the content is my personal story: how I went from terrified to TEDx. I will take you from my first disastrous presentation to my TEDx talk experience and on to the amazing events that have happened since.

How to get the most from this book

You can't learn presentation skills if you only read the techniques: you need to apply them. So at the end of each chapter is a practical exercise. Therefore to get the most out of this book:

1. have a specific presentation in mind that you need to develop and
2. apply the exercises to that presentation.

So for example, during the chapter on the goal of a presentation, ask yourself, what is the goal of *your* presentation?

If you don't have a presentation coming up, think about how you would have improved your previous presentation. Or pretend you've been asked to give your ideal presentation: the perfect topic to your dream audience. Use this book to create that presentation. And who knows? You might just make it happen!

Presentation Planner

You'll need to make notes in these exercises to prepare your presentation. To make this as easy for you as possible, I've also created the **Speak Inspire Empower Presentation Planner** which can also be ordered online. It contains the summaries and exercises from all these chapters so that you can quickly and easily create new presentations.

Coming up...

You've seen bad presentations; you may even have given some of them (I know I have, as you will see in the next few pages). Why are they so bad? And what is it that great speakers do that makes their speeches[1] so amazing?

For the most part, it's not something they are born with - it's something they *learn*.

In the next chapter, you will learn why so many presentations are so boring. But more importantly, you will learn the simple formula for making great speeches and presentations: the 3 Es.

---

[1] I use the words "presentation" and "speech" deliberately interchangeably, since they are fundamentally the same. This book will help you with all forms of public speaking, including pitches.

Summary

Developing your presentation skills
will improve your:

1. **Confidence**: if you can speak confidently in front of a group, you can speak confidently anywhere.
2. **Career**: you will be seen as *the* expert on any topic you speak on.
3. **Charisma**: you will be able to inspire a group to follow your lead.

Can you learn presentation skills from a book? No, not unless you put what you learn into practice. That's why every content chapter has a practical exercise.

After finishing each chapter, use these exercises to improve your public speaking skills. You can use the dedicated Presentation Planner (see above) for this. This planner contains all the summaries and exercises for each chapter and gives you space to write. So it's ideal for creating speeches or presentations.

Otherwise, just grab a notepad and write your answers down. And complete the indented sentences in italics.

When you are preparing for a specific presentation, you can use these exercises to create and develop your talk.

Exercise

From chess players to Olympic champions, many successful people start working towards their goal by first *visualising* achieving it.

So first take a moment to consider this: if I had a magic wand and could guarantee your speech or presentation would be a huge success, what would happen? How would your audience respond to your presentation? What do they *do*?

Does your audience applaud? Do they give you a standing ovation? If it's a work presentation, do your colleagues and managers say things like, *"Well done!"*, *"That was inspirational!"* and *"That was great, I didn't know you had that in you"*?

If it's at a conference, you walk offstage with your audience's applause ringing in your ears. Do people come up to you afterwards to congratulate you and ask you about your topic?

Write down how your audience ideally responds. Start with this text:

> *After I give my presentation, my audience will ideally respond by...*

And how do you *feel* at the end of this ideal response to your presentation? Relieved? Elated? Excited? Write down how you feel at the end of your successful presentation.

My speech goes down even better than I'd hoped! After I give this great speech, I feel...

Terrified

"The human brain starts working the moment you are born and never stops until you stand up to speak in public."
George Jessel - actor

What do you remember from your school days? I have a few memories, but one stands out. It was a painful moment which made me fearful for decades and can still affect me today.

Our teacher asked us to prepare a presentation on any topic to deliver in front of the class. He told us we should speak for, *"just a couple of minutes"*.

At home, I started to prepare. I had absolutely zero idea how to give a presentation. So I did what any untrained presenter does in that situation: I created a *data dump*. I made a list of all the interesting facts on my chosen topic.

When I say, *"interesting facts"*, I mean all the facts that I found interesting. Like any untrained presenter, I hadn't given much thought to my audience!

The next day I walked off to school carrying a poster from my bedroom wall. I had hardly slept because all I could think about was my having to speak in front of the class. During the rest of the school day, I could not concentrate on anything: the forthcoming presentation filled my mind.

I was already feeling scared: as a 13-year-old boy, the last thing you want is to look bad in front of your friends. And here I was about to be the centre of attention, have every pair of eyes in the room focus on *me* for two minutes. *"Scared"* is not the right word; I was *terrified*.

The lesson began. Our teacher was a man in his 50s with shoulder-length hair and an otherwise bald head. He had a slow, dull voice and every sentence contained the phrase, *"in fact"*. Looking back now as an adult, I could have realised this man was not an expert in presenting.

"Today is, in fact, the first day to hear your presentations. Who of you would, in fact, like to go first?"

I didn't *want* to go at all, in fact. But I wanted to get it over and done with. This was the first day: there would probably be several days over the next two or three weeks before the whole class of 30 would have had their turn. If I went first, I could start sleeping again and not have to think about this anymore. Or so I thought.

I raised my hand and was called forward. And so, with every pair of eyes on me, I made the long walk from the back of the class to the front. With shaking hands, I unrolled my poster to reveal my chosen subject: the Lockheed SR-71 Blackbird aircraft.

Still shaking and (I was told later by my friends), going completely white, I rattled off all the facts I knew about the Blackbird: it's top speed, why it was black, etc. And when I was done, I abruptly stopped.

Two minutes had gone by. I had survived. All I had to do now was listen to our hippy teacher give, in fact, his feedback and then I could sit down, relax and watch my friends take their turns.

That was my plan. But that's not how it happened. Instead, I heard this, *"That wasn't, in fact, very long. Could you talk some more about the, in fact, Blackbird?"*

To me, this was a living nightmare! I'd prepared two minutes' worth of material as he'd told us. And now he wanted more? What was I going to say?!

I think I managed to recall a couple of other facts. Then I went quiet. He looked, in fact, disappointed and told me I could sit down.

As I sat down, still shaking, I felt two things: *relief* that it was over and *convinced* that presenting was not for me.

I gave at least one other presentation at school, this time about the space shuttle. It went slightly better than the Blackbird talk because I got one of my friends to ask me a prepared question[2], a trick I later repeated at my TEDx talk.

However, I had allowed a **limiting belief** to settle in my brain. I was convinced I could never speak confidently in front of a group. And so I avoided every opportunity to do so, hurting my career and confidence in the process.

That limiting belief would stay stuck in my brain, feeding off my self-confidence like a parasite, for the next 15 years.

It had taken just two minutes for that belief

---

[2] *"How do the astronauts go to the toilet?"* The whole class of teenagers laughed. You've got to know your audience...

to take root in my brain. But a decade and a half later, something amazing would happen for it to start to loosen its grip...

What is a limiting belief?

A limiting belief is something you believe about yourself which prevents you from achieving your potential. It is untrue. But because you believe it, it determines the boundaries of what you are prepared to do. It limits you.

Unless you call it out and face up to it, a limiting belief becomes a self-imposed prison.

Do you have a limiting belief? Take a moment to consider what you believe you cannot do.

Maybe you believe, as I did, that you cannot speak in front of a group. As you read this book, notice how that belief disappears. It will be replaced with a *conviction* that **you too can present**.

I believe that *everyone* has a unique and powerful message within them. But sometimes that message is locked away. That lock is made up of fear, based on a wrong belief (that you can't present) and a lack of skills. Both of these are rooted in a lack of knowledge.

This book gives you that knowledge. This book is the **key** to that lock.

The 3 Es: why are most presentations so boring and how can you make a great presentation?

"All the great speakers were bad speakers at first."
Ralph Waldo Emerson – philosopher

Prepare for your reprogramming

This book will forever change how you view presentations. From now on, when you see a boring presentation, you will think, *"Why are they doing that? Great presenting is so easy! Why don't they attend a training course and learn how to present? Why don't they read a book on presentation skills?"* (Preferably this one, of course...)

I will prove this to you in the next few minutes. First, take a moment to think about *the very best* presentations you've ever seen. What made them so good? Seriously, put the book down and consider this. It will help you greatly in what follows.

Done? OK.

When I ask this question in my workshop, here are some of the answers I get:

- the person spoke with *passion*
- they made jokes
- it was personal
- there was a powerful message
- it was easy to understand
- it was memorable
- they somehow kept us listening / kept our attention

and so on. Sometimes people will say, *"It was short"*. Then someone else will give an example of a longer talk which still kept their attention.

And then I ask them what they think of the presentations at their workplace. At this moment, the group usually starts laughing and says, *"Nothing like that!"*.

Why is that? What are so many work presentations missing? The answer is: great presentations have The Three Es! But most business presentations often only have one E.

What are these three Es? Let's look at them one at a time.

The Teacher

Albert Einstein - Theoretical physicist

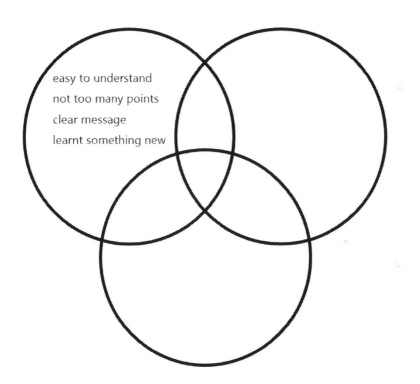

easy to understand
not too many points
clear message
learnt something new

What is the first E? It's all about the *content*: ensuring people learn something but not too much. The answer?

Education

Yes, there needs to be *some content* in your talk, the audience needs to learn something new. However, it's not a *lack* of content that most presentations suffer from. The problem for most presentations is an *overflow* of content.

I blame PowerPoint. People seem to assume:

"Presentation = PowerPoint".

This. Is. Not. True.

When it's time to prepare their presentation, what do most presenters do? They open their laptops, start PowerPoint and begin to type... and they only end when they've created a .ppt file full of *everything they know on the subject.*

- In
- an
- endless
- series
- of
- bullet
- points

On

- slide
- after
- slide
- after
- slide

Are you feeling it? It's so BORING!

The problem is that PowerPoint enables people to cram loads of information onto a slide in the most boring way possible - and then repeat that through 89 slides; which they want to get through in 20 minutes.

It's information diarrhoea. And you're the pot they're squatting over[3].

Besides, if all the information is in the slides... what is the point of presenting it? Just send the info around. At least then we can then ~~delete it~~ read it in our own time.

So please remember this rule: **Do not try to present documentation!**

Yes, you need *some* content, some Education. But not as much as you'd think. How much content is the right amount? We will cover that a bit later.

---

[3] There will be a few analogies in this book. I can't promise they will all be that great.

The Jester

*"When dealing with people, remember you are not dealing
with creatures of logic, but creatures of emotion."*
Dale Carnegie - author & trainer

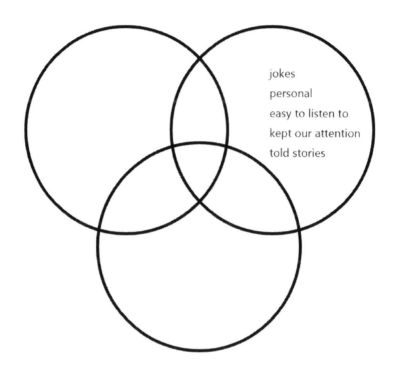

jokes

personal

easy to listen to

kept our attention

told stories

What is this E? It's about keeping you listening, ensuring
that you are hanging on the edge of your seat, desperate
to hear what is coming next.

This E is:

Entertainment

This E makes you *want* to hear more of the talk and are sorry when it is finished! When has that ever happened at your work? Let me guess: almost *never*.

But what do I mean with entertainment? Am I expecting you to juggle? Well, that would keep attention for a while, but No. The techniques I will teach you are much simpler. And they're coming later.

Why is Entertainment so important? Because you've got to keep their attention! If your audience stops listening, it doesn't matter how great your content (Education) is - nobody will hear your amazing message.

This has become far worse in the last decade. Nowadays, everyone carries smartphones (I'm writing this part of the book on a smartphone!). So if your presentation is boring, what's to stop them from checking out of your presentation and checking into their social media?

Fellow presenters, here is the bitter truth: **it's your PowerPoint versus their Smartphones**. And as the next generation comes into the marketplace, people who've almost been born with a phone in their hand, this problem is just going to get worse.

Unless you are prepared radically to change your approach to presenting, their smartphones will win. But since you're reading this book I believe you're open to making this change. In the upcoming chapters, I will show you how you can present to keep your audience's attention.

The Superhero

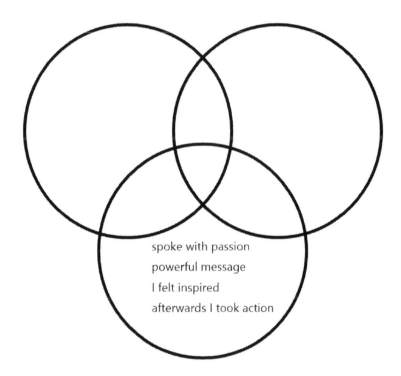

spoke with passion

powerful message

I felt inspired

afterwards I took action

This E is related to the Great Unanswered Question. By that I mean, the question that most presentations leave unanswered. And yet, this is the question that *every* audience member has on their minds during *every* presentation.

And that question is:

WII4ME?

Or: What's In It For Me?

You MUST answer this question in your presentation. You must give them a reason to listen to you. This is related to the Goal of your presentation, which we will look at very soon.

So what is this E? It's probably the reason you bought this book.

Empowerment

Your presentation should *change* your audience! Your talk should **enable them to do something new**. Nothing less. That's empowerment. You give them the **power** to do something they could not before hearing your words. Why is this? And how can you implement this in *your* presentation? That's coming up in the next chapter.

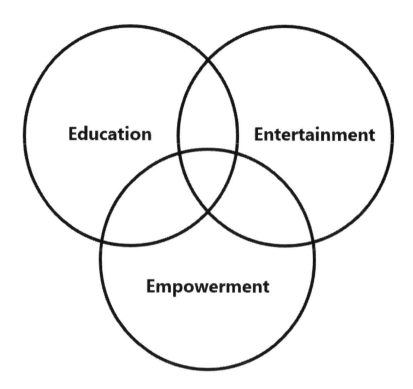

So why are so many presentations so mind-numbingly boring?

"Words have incredible power. They can make people's
hearts soar, or they can make people's hearts sore."
Dr Mardy Grothe - psychologist, speaker & author

Why? Because they've only got Education. That's it. Tons and tons of education. Slide after slide of potentially great content but it is hidden behind what seems like billions of bland, brain-destroying bullet points. Concealed somewhere in these presentations is *good stuff*. But you, the poor listener, have to search for it. It's like looking for a piece of hay in a whole stack of needles... and nearly as painful.

Most presentations in the workplace are like this:

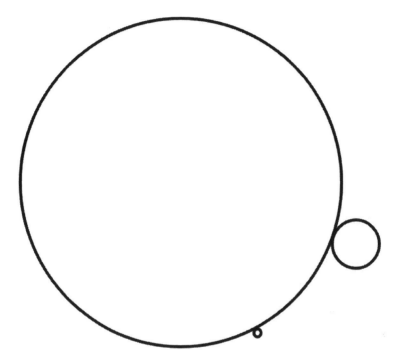

They have lots of education, a tiny bit of entertainment[4] and no empowerment. If you are in the audience, you leave

---

[4] When the presenter trips over the laptop power cord, causing the laptop to crash on the floor and the beamer to start flashing. There is no Education in this part, but it gets your attention and therefore we will generously classify it as *"Entertainment"*.

the presentation Unchanged, Unmoved and Uninspired: the 3 Us are the opposite of the 3 Es!

Coming up...

If the goal is not to tell your audience everything you know on a topic, what should the goal of your presentation be? That's answered in our next chapter!

Summary

Every presentation should contain the 3 Es:

1. **Education**: some content, but much less than you are used to.
2. **Entertainment**: something to keep you listening.
3. **Empowerment**: how will your audience be changed?

Exercise

Earlier in this chapter you thought about the very best presentations you've attended and what made them so good.

Now draw the three interlocking circles on a piece of paper with Education, Entertainment and Empowerment each next to one circle. Write the best qualities in the appropriate circles, for example write, *"Told personal stories"* in the Entertainment circle.

Take a few moments to think about your talk. Draw another three circles. Write down any ideas you have that will fit into each of these three circles. Don't worry about getting it perfect: focus on generating ideas.

The day it all changed

"By changing our thoughts, we can change our lives."
Dale Carnegie - author & trainer

Fast forward to my late twenties. I'm now married, living in The Netherlands and working in IT. The company I was working for[5] is great at investing in training. So they encouraged me to go on an *"Advanced Leadership"* course by Remco Claassen[6]. This was a powerful course which would be worthy of another book.

But what struck me is this: throughout the whole three and a half-day course, Remco kept our attention completely! The full days started at 9 am and went on until 10 pm - and yet we were hooked!

---

[5] Sioux, https://www.sioux.eu
[6] https://remcoclaassen.nl

I remember cycling home each evening on the dark winter roads, being physically exhausted but mentally alive! My brain was buzzing with all that I had heard. How had he done that?

A couple of months later, the mystery was revealed. Remco gave a 12-hour workshop (over three half-days) called: *"Speaking with Impact!!"* He started by saying, *"In this course, I will become completely transparent. You will see all the techniques and sneaky tricks I use to keep your attention."*

And we did. These 12 or so hours changed my life. I learnt, for the first time, why so many presentations are *so boring* (because of too much Education). I learnt how to speak in a way that keeps people *listening* (Entertainment). And I learnt how to inspire people to *action* (Empowerment). Some of the ideas in my TEDx talk, particularly about the importance of keeping attention and how to do so, came straight from Remco.

Over the next decade, I started to put these techniques into practice. In the meantime, I learnt more about not only presentations but also persuasion. My presentations started to get better and better.

Though the nerves have never left me, they've got more under control. I've spoken at conferences and, when I do, I always get very high reviews; consistently the best of all the speakers.

And it all started with that workshop. I want you to take two things away from this:

1. You CAN present. I know, I've already said that. But I want to make sure you get the message. You can present and, in the few hours you invest in reading this book and practicing the exercises, you will learn how.
2. If you have a limiting belief, you can remove it. It might take coaching or training. But please do it - become the person you were meant to be.

Sometimes life gives you a *defining moment:* an experience which changes your life. That presentation skills workshop was one of those moments. But at the time I had no idea just how life-changing it would be...

The goal of your presentation (or why should I give you an hour of my life I will never get back?)

"If you don't know what you want to achieve in your presentation your audience never will."
Harvey Diamond - author

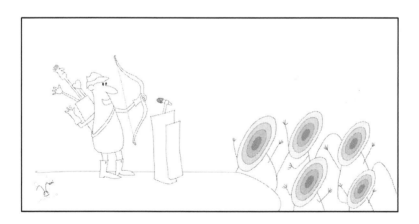

The soul-sucking monster does not exist only in science-fiction horror movies. It's also your well-meaning, otherwise very charming colleague. Armed with PowerPoint[7].

But right now your colleague might be reading this book and thinking of *your* last presentation. So now let's make the first major step in improving your next presentation.

What is the very first thing you need to consider when preparing a presentation?

The answer is: what is the GOAL? Why are you giving this presentation? What do you hope to achieve?

You wouldn't start a business without a goal, right? Heck, you probably wouldn't do anything without a goal, whether it is a conscious goal or unconscious. But presentations? We'll happily stand in front of a group without THE FAINTEST IDEA what we want to achieve!

---

[7] People ask, *"If you could go back in time and kill baby Hitler, would you do so?"* A far more humane solution to preventing WW2 and the Holocaust would have been to give him MS PowerPoint. Can you imagine that? First slide, three bullet points:

- Invade Poland
- Take over Europe
- Establish Master Race

Audience response? *"ZZZZzzzzzz"* and *"Give it a rest, Adolf!"* History would have been entirely different.

But what is a goal for a presentation? What does that even look like?

First, what is not a goal?

Not a goal

Recently a senior manager came to me for help. He was asked to give a five-minute presentation to other senior managers. He started by telling me a bit about what he wanted to say.

I interrupted him, *"Sorry, but could you please tell me, what is the **goal** of your presentation?"* He looked blank for a moment, then looked away to think. After a few seconds, he said, *"I want to create awareness on this topic."* I said, *"I'd like you to think BIGGER. What would you like people TO DO as a result of your presentation?"*

What is a presentation goal?

"To change the future, you need to disturb the present."
William Booth - Salvation Army co-founder

Your presentation should not be built around content: what you know about a topic. Instead, it should be built on the needs of your audience - the customer of your presentation.

Now let's look at the goal and break it down into three parts based on your audience:

- what you want them to **remember**
- what you want them to **feel**
- what you want them to **do**

In other words, remember the 3Hs: **Head**, **Heart** & **Hands!**

Let's take them one at a time.

What should they remember?

It's the end of your presentation. The audience begins to leave. I'm standing at the door and I ask everyone the same question: *"What was that presentation about?"*

What are they going to say?

What do you *want* them to say?

Typically when I coach someone, the answer to the first question starts with the same word: *Something.*

- *Something* about my project
- *Something* about our sales forecasts
- *Something* management blah-blah

If you knew how little people can recall from a presentation, you would weep (especially when it's *your* presentation!). And that's *right after* the presentation is given! What about the next day? The next week? A month later? Six months later? The sad truth is: often 90% of your presentation is completely forgotten before you've powered down your laptop.

How much can people realistically remember? The harsh reality is: people can typically remember a maximum of **three points** from your presentation.

So, when I ask people leaving your presentation, *"what was that presentation about?"*, your goal should be that everyone mentions the same three points of *content* (Education). So ask yourself: what are the three main points that your audience should remember?

How should they feel?

"They may forget what you said, but they will never forget how you made them feel."
Carl W. Buehner - Latter Day Saints church official

I often ask this question in my workshops: *"How do you feel at the end of a typical business presentation?"* The answers are *always* the same: most presentations leave people in one of three states:

- **B**ored
- **A**sleep
- **D**ead

This *must* change! We've got to stop making **BAD** presentations. But we've also got to stop *accepting* them. Decide today:

1. you're going to finish this book so that
2. you will only give *great* presentations from now on

But back to the *feeling*. Let's think big. How do you want people to *feel* after your presentation?

You might be thinking, *"But Mark, this is a business presentation! Why should they feel anything? As long as I don't bore them, isn't that enough?"*

No, it's not, not by a long way. We can do much better. We want people to **remember** our presentations and **do** something as a result. People are not machines. They *remember* when they *feel* something and they *do* when they are *emotionally moved* to action.

Inspired

When you make people *feel* something, you can change the world. *"I have a dream!"* Those four words of Martin Luther King Jr contain no content (Education). But they are red hot: they inspired a nation to change and hence changed the world.

So, how do you want people to feel at the end of your presentation?

You want to make people feel **inspired!** They should feel that they *need to take action*. Action to improve the world, to improve *their* world. They should understand that there is a problem they must solve and, with the Education in your presentation (particularly the three main points), that they have the power to solve it.

Occasionally, feeling inspired is not enough. If the problem is so big or so urgent, you may want your audience to feel *anger*.

Angry

"If you think you are too small to make an impact try going to bed with a mosquito in the room."
Ekaterina Walter - speaker

If you are working for a charity, e.g. **Light for the World**, you may want people to feel anger that humans, just like you and me, do not have access to relatively basic health care. Or if you support the **International Justice Mission**, you will want people to feel anger that some people are being bought and sold like property. If you are moved by **WhizzKidz**, you may want people to feel anger when children do not get the same opportunities as their friends simply because of a disability. Or if you are speaking on behalf of **Compassion** or **World Vision**, you may want people to feel angry that some children do not have anything like the same opportunities that yours have. And don't get me started on how moved you want your audience to feel if you speak on behalf of **War Child**.

These examples are high octane emotion. But you may want to make people at your work feel angry at wasted resources, especially wasted talent[8] or missed opportunities.

Anger is an emotion which demands action. But beware: if you chose to use anger, you can't leave it there. You must add inspiration. Anger and inspiration together prepare the way for your message. What is that message? It's when you clearly show, no, **tell** people exactly what they must do.

What should they do?

You want people to remember three main points and to feel inspired. But inspired to do what? What do you want them to *do* with the information in your presentation?

You may be surprised at the question: why should your presentation audience do anything? You were just told to present something about your project; all they have to do is be bodily present in the same room (mentally present is often entirely optional).

But wait, that's the *old* way of thinking, where Education is everything! We want people to be Empowered, so they

---

[8] This is part of my inspiration for writing this book: many people's talents are hidden because they do not know how to express themselves effectively in front of a group.

have to *do something* as a result. They must not leave your presentation unchanged!

So, what do you want them to do? At the *very least*, your desired action can be *"Contact me to find out more"*, *"Let me know if you have any feedback"* or *"Remember these three points!"* But those examples are pretty weak - you are not presenting so that you can give them even more *Education*. You want them to get into action.

Therefore I encourage you to **think big**. Start with the *ideal* answer. In the *ideal world*, what will people do as a result of your presentation?

- adopt a new way of working?
- go to your website and sign up for your workshop?
- give you funding?
- join your project?
- queue up to buy your product?

Your three points of education will all be linked to this action.

To be clear: that *action* is the **real goal** of your presentation. *Everything else* is to make sure that this action is carried out successfully. And in the time after your presentation, that *action* will be the only lasting, real change.

When I say action, you might think of a *physical* action. But it might be a mental one: for example, a decision to *change one's attitude*. An attitude change might be more significant than a physical action because attitude can influence *multiple physical actions* in the future.

Let's say you have to present an organisational change. Your call to action might be to embrace the change (we'll see an example of this later).

But how do you *motivate* people to do this? Whether people welcome the change, or resist it, will be strongly influenced by how they *feel* about it, which in turn is influenced by how they feel about your presentation. That's why *inspiration* precedes *empowerment*. It's also why, as you'll see later, clarifying the *Problem* must come before the *Solution*. Before you can tell people why they need to move to the new state, they must be convinced they can no longer accept the status quo.

How do you inspire your audience to act? We'll talk much more about this later, when we talk about confidence, stories and persuasion. How do you deliver your call to action? We'll also come to that later when we talk about how to end your presentation.

Coming up...

Once you've chosen your goal, by thinking about your audience's head, heart and hands, how do you prepare for your presentation? What do you need to do to ensure that, when you stand in front of your audience, you deliver a powerful presentation? That's coming up next.

Summary

Remember: head, heart & hands.

Your **goal** should be:

1. to **speak** three main points your audience must remember,
2. to **inspire** your audience to act and
3. to **empower** your audience to do something new.

Exercise

What are the three things you want people to remember from your presentation? If you have been asked to do this presentation, check with the person making the request. Does your goal match their expectations?

*Here are the three things I want people to **remember** after my presentation:*

1.
2.
3.

*After my presentation, I want people to **feel**:*

*This is what I want people to **do** after my presentation (and when I want them to do it):*

Popeye moment

"The single biggest problem in communication is the illusion that it has taken place."
George Bernard Shaw - playwright

Fast forward another 10 years. I've been presenting better and better each time, gradually gaining confidence as I learn and apply new techniques, especially those I learnt from Remco. I've been speaking in-company and at conferences. Though I've remained nervous, the feedback I've been getting has been consistently improving.

At the same time, I've seen my colleagues struggling through their presentations. They are often really smart people[9], doing great work. But they simply cannot communicate it

---

[9] I live in Eindhoven, a high tech hub often referred to as *"the smartest place on the planet"*.

effectively. They go from slide to slide, all filled with bullet points and lots of text, without any clear goal or message.

The frustrating part for me is that I realise how easy it is to solve this. With one day of presentation skills training, these messages could become clear, focused and fun to listen to. And the audience would leave inspired by a call to action. It would be a win / win for the presenter and the audience.

In 2013 my frustration became too much for me. I was then contracted to work at ASML[10] via my employer, TMC[11]. You need to know just how smart the average ASML-er is: recently someone said in front of a group of about 300 ASML staff, *"There are probably more doctorates in this room than people!"* and he was only half-joking. ASML recruits the smartest people from all over the world to work in the smartest region on the planet.

So imagine my feeling when I saw an intelligent senior manager at ASML stand in front of a group of these super-smart people and... read out slides. *Seriously?!* That was his

[10] https://www.asml.com
[11] https://tmc-employeneurship.com

whole presentation: slides of text displayed on a giant screen and read out, line-by-line, to us.

This, and many similar presentations, brought me to my Popeye moment: like the cartoon character, I thought, *"That's all I can stands, I can't stands no more!"*

I went out determined to change this. (Well, it was either change myself or change the world, and the latter seemed easier.) I started to compare what I had just seen with some of the most inspiring people who'd ever given a speech. They were like opposite ends of the speaking spectrum.

And that gave me an idea. I remember exactly where I was, walking past the ASML reception, when an idea hit me. I could make exactly this point in a funny way: I would deliver a famous speech in the *"engineering management PowerPoint"* style to show how they are ruining their message. But which speech? And how could I get an audience?

How to prepare

"It takes one hour of preparation for each minute of presentation time."
Wayne Burgraff - philosopher

You've seen what we are aiming for: not just Education (facts) but also Entertainment (so that people listen) and Empowerment (action!). And we've identified our goal: people should remember three things, have an action to do after the presentation and feel inspired to do it.

Now imagine you are sitting down to prepare your presentation. How should you prepare? What steps should you take to ensure that, when you stand in front of your audience, you have a great message that you can deliver with confidence?

Let's start with the bad news. You can't do this in just an hour, or even in half a day. You will need about **an hour of preparation for every minute presenting**.

That's a rule of thumb. It may be more or less, depending on:

- how much experience you have at presenting and how good you are,
- how well you know the topic,

- how well you know your audience and
- if you are reusing your own material or creating it from scratch (if it's the latter, you may well need two hours per minute).

So now for some good news:

"90% of how well the talk will go is determined before the speaker steps on the platform."
Somers White - management consultant

In other words, if you make this time investment upfront, doing the presentation itself is *"just"* the last 10%.

So the preparation, and hence this chapter, is crucial.

How do you prepare? Let's start with a mind map.

Mind map

When I am preparing to give a presentation, I start by creating a mind map. Here is an example of a mind map for part of this chapter:

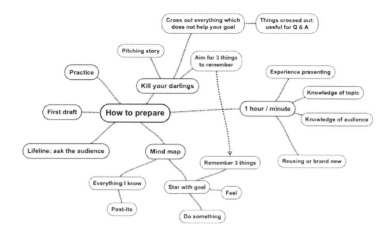

For a presentation, I start by drawing a circle in the centre of the paper[12]. In this circle I write my goal:

- the three things people should **remember**
- what I want them to **do**
- how I want them to **feel**

Next, I add everything I know about this topic. Obviously, I don't write literally *everything* but just the main groups of topics: I try to group ideas as much as possible. Tip: if you write your points on Post-its you can easily move them around to group them.

---

[12] I'm assuming you will use paper and pen. Great electronic versions are also available. I really like SimpleMind for the iPad which I find very user friendly.

Typically the first draft of the mind map will take about 30 minutes. I say, *"the first draft"* because this is an iterative process. As you discover more about your presentation and the needs of your audience, you may change your goals and update the mind map. This is normal.

Next comes the hardest, and yet most important, part of your preparation...

Kill your darlings

"The secret of being a bore is to tell everything."
Voltaire - author & philosopher

My wife (who also trains people in presentation skills - she's my strongest competitor!) taught me this phrase: *Kill Your Darlings!*[13]. It refers to this tough step: on your mind map, cross out *everything which does not help your goal*.

Sounds simple but, as a speaker myself, I know how painful this is because these points are great! They are really important to you: they're *your darlings!* And yet, you have to kill them. Why? First, because they don't help your goal. And secondly, because they are simply too much for your audience - you are in danger of *educating them to death*.

_____

[13] The irony that *my wife* taught me, *"kill your darlings"* is not lost on me.

So, strike out as much as you can. We're aiming for three main things people must remember (see the previous chapter). But you may not yet be left with only three major points. If so, don't worry, you will have chances to kill other darlings, particularly when you start practicing out loud.

Let me tell you a story which will help you know what to cut out. I was once coaching a group of people preparing two - minute presentations (personal pitches) to potential employers. During the practice run, all of them went over two minutes. One woman spoke for four minutes, double the allowed time! She asked me what to cut out. I replied, *"It seemed to me that you spoke with the most passion and energy at the start of your talk and at the end, is that right?"* She confirmed this. So I said, *"Then use those parts and cut out the middle!"* The "middle" was mainly listing facts and qualifications, some of which could easily be dropped: this was a pitch to get an interview, not to give her whole CV.

So after you've cut out the *"easy stuff"*, those darlings that don't help your goal, then focus on keeping whatever gives *you* the most energy when you speak about it. Then cross out the darlings which don't give you energy: those that drain you or make you feel weak. Keep the darlings that will make you feel stronger as you present them.

What happens to all those darlings you cut out? You might have invested time in researching them, only later to choose to remove them. Was it a waste of your time? Not necessarily, because they may come up in a question and answer session at the end of your talk.

Use your lifeline: ask the audience

"Designing a presentation without an audience in mind is like writing a love letter and addressing it: To Whom It May Concern."
Ken Haemer - author

The game show *"Who Wants To Be A Millionaire?"* has a number of so-called *"lifelines"* to help contestants get the correct answer. One of those is *"Ask the Audience"* where the contestant, who doesn't know the answer to a question, can ask the audience what they think is the right answer. *"Ask the Audience"* is also a valuable lifeline in presenting!

So as part of your preparation, consult your audience. If you want to sell a product or service, you would want to check the needs of your customer before creating it, wouldn't you? So shouldn't we do the same with presentations? After all, these are also our *"products"* that we are creating for our customer (the audience). But how often do we check our presentations with our customers, really?

What's the best way to ask your audience? Let's say you have to present to 30 colleagues. I don't suggest you go and speak to *all* of them. Instead, select at least three and have a one-on-one coffee with each of them[14]. Tell them that you've been asked to give a presentation to their group on this topic (here you tell them the topic name) and that you'd value their advice[15]. Then say, *"What would you like to hear?"*

Note down their advice. After this, you can even show them your mind map (together with the areas you've crossed out) to stimulate their thoughts, including showing them your goal and three points. You should do this *after* they give their advice, not before. Why? Because you don't want to limit their ideas by focusing them on what you are considering.

Apart from getting great ideas and feedback on what you are preparing, there is another advantage: since they buy into your preparation, they are much more likely to buy into your final presentation. They are more likely to support the message of the presentation if, say, there are hostile questions. They want you to succeed because it's partly their presentation. It's as if, by consulting them, they've bought shares in your presentation!

---

[14] This is the Dutch way. Replace *"have a coffee"* with your culturally appropriate low threshold, informal meeting.
[15] According to Dr Robert Cialdini (in his book, *Pre-Suasion: A Revolutionary Way to Influence and Persuade*), you should ask for *"advice"*, not *"opinion"*. Opinion puts people into a more introspective state (focusing on themselves); you want them focusing on your presentation!

That's all fine if your audience is colleagues, people you can easily approach. What about senior management or people who attend a conference?

Senior management

If you've ever been asked to present to senior management, e.g. board members, you will know that you cannot just drop in on them to show them your mind map. They tend to have full schedules: working days (and evenings) planned weeks in advance. So, what can you do?

You can't get *their* time but you can get the time of people who know them. There are three categories of people you can approach:

- Other managers who know them, typically between you and them in the hierarchy. They may also be willing to review your presentation.
- Personal Assistants: they can often warn you of potential *"landmines"*; for example, if a manager has an allergy to a certain buzzword. If you are nice to them, they may plan you in at a good time, for example at the end of the working day where the manager might give you more time because there is no meeting directly after.
- Senior colleagues, and by senior I mean people who are often older and have met *"management"* before. I'm not talking about people who *complain* about management (stay well away) but people who have given these presentations before and / or met these managers previously - the *influencers* in the

64

company. They may also be willing to review your presentation.

Conferences

Here, you do not necessarily know *who* will be attending let alone what their needs are. Furthermore, you are likely to be speaking to a group of 100 or 200 people - how can you identify all *their* needs?

As with speaking to a group at your workplace, you don't need to take *everyone* into account. You are looking to find out what the *typical* attendee needs to hear.

My best advice is to contact the conference organisers. If they have invited you or at least approved your submission (if you took the initiative to approach them[16]), they will want you to be successful. And they know their delegates well. So as part of your preparation, ask the organisers if you can book a (video) call to get their feedback on your plan for your presentation.

---

[16] And if you did, good on you! Speaking at a conference will increase your visibility, self-confidence and give you a great learning experience.

Practice

Should you practice your speech? My answer is: yes, definitely, with one very rare exception which I will come to in a moment.

Why should you practice? And how often? To answer the second question first, my *"rule of thumb"* is that you should practice out loud, preferably in the room where you will give the presentation, at least ten times. This is part of your 1 hour preparation / 1 minute presenting. So why practice - and why ten times?

In my experience, the first five times I am just getting the *story* right: I'm getting the presentation in the right order and killing a few more darlings[17]. The next five times I already know the talk is pretty settled. Now I'm learning it to make sure I can speak without looking at my notes if possible. Here I may tweak a few phrases and add a few jokes. Important: don't design the talk around the jokes! Create the talk and *then* decide if there is anything funny you can say. This is also the phase to add a STAR moment (see later) if you haven't already.

---

[17] I always dread my first *"out loud"* practice. Even though it is in an empty room, I put it off as long as possible! Why? Because it will be terrible! Everything will be in the wrong order and I will say too much. But this is a necessary step. If I didn't practice it out loud first, this terrible version would be my *"go live"* presentation!

Take every opportunity to practice: in the car, in the shower, ... each time you practice your words will flow more easily. And when you come to speak in front of your audience you will feel much more confident.

Should you always practice ten times? No, that's a rough number to give you an idea. It can be more or fewer.

- Practice fewer than ten times if you know the subject well, the presentation is not so important (a small group of close colleagues) or you really don't have the time (when it's 10 o'clock and you've been asked to present at 11...).
- Practice more than ten times for an important presentation, like a presentation to senior management or at a conference.

When I practice, I time myself and I write down how long it takes. After several practices, I will have the duration of each written down. This shows me not only how many times I've practiced but also if my talk is getting longer or shorter - and therefore whether I have to kill more darlings.

Always check in advance with your host how long your presentation should take *and stick to it.* One of the worst things you can do is go over time. I once saw someone speak too long at a pitch event. The host asked him to wrap up. Instead he kept going... the host asked him again. He still kept going. What do you think the effect was on the audience? They went from laughing to hostile in a few moments. There is almost no better way to alienate your public than to speak longer than the allowed time. And the other speakers were pretty mad too that he ate into their time and created a hostile atmosphere for their talks. Stick to your allotted time.

Practice the whole talk. But especially practice the start and the end. These are the parts that have to be the strongest. If you have a strong start, you will feel more confident and your audience will listen better to the rest of your talk. If you have a strong end, you will leave a great impression with your audience.

I said that you should preferably practice in the room where you will give the presentation. Why is that? There are many benefits:

- You get to test the equipment.
  - If you are using slides, does your laptop have the right connector to the projector? Do the slides show up as you expect, or has the aspect ratio changed?[18] If you use video, is the sound OK or will you need to bring external speakers?
  - If you are using a flip chart, can what you write be read everywhere in the room?
- You can explore the space. Will you have a lectern? Do you have space to walk left and right in front of

---

[18] I've seen so many presentations where this has not been tested: the slides look terrible: words are moved around or overlapping... This makes the speaker look bad and kills their self-confidence. It's easily avoided by testing in advance.

your audience? How far can you approach your audience?

- You can picture the audience in your mind. If you've done your research, you know who they are. I like to imagine them all looking disinterested, scowling up at me with their arms crossed! This helps me to give extra energy. In my mind, I think: Challenge Accepted! And I speak with more enthusiasm to fire them up!

The exception

And the exception? Who shouldn't practice? There are some people who are natural presenters. They aren't afraid when they stand on a stage: they own it from the first moment! They are spontaneous, creative, funny and inspirational. They are also very rare.

If you are one of these people, you may feel that practicing your talk robs you of that magical spontaneity you have and therefore harms your talk. In that case, I would advise you only to practice your talk if you need to get the timing right. And do this in the room where you will deliver the presentation, for the reasons mentioned above.

Since you are a creative person, the practice might also give you new ideas for your presentation and especially a STAR moment. But that's all. By all means, apply the tips in this book if they help you - just don't let them constrain you. You have a special gift - please keep sharing it with us.

Coming up...

Now, what do you think is the most important part of your presentation? And how can you be sure you get that part right? That's the subject of the next chapter.

Summary

Prepare by:

1. Mind mapping what you *could* talk about, with your goal at the centre.
2. Killing your darlings: remove *everything* that does not help your goal.
3. Asking the audience: speak with people in advance - what are they wanting from your talk?
4. Practice, practice, practice,...

Exercise

Using the goal you identified for your presentation in the previous chapter:

1. Create your own mind map for your presentation. Start by putting the three-part goal from the previous chapter in the middle.
2. Cross off everything which does not help your goal.
3. Who would be the audience for your presentation? Can you speak with a few potential audience members and get their feedback on your mind map? Should you add anything? Could you cross anything else off? Perhaps you even need to reconsider your goal. That's OK: this is an iterative process as you discover the ideal presentation for your audience.

"

An evening at TMC

"Hide not your talents, they for use were made. What's a sundial in the shade?"
Benjamin Franklin - writer, politician &
American Founding Father

In 2013, I decided that I wanted to help people to develop their presentation skills by teaching them the techniques I had learnt. It was like I was passing on the gift Remco and others had given me. The obvious place to start was with people like me: technical people in the Eindhoven area.

So, I booked a room at our company (TMC) office and we sent around an email to the whole company (then about 600 people):

Subject: How to deliver a great presentation?

The ability to present to a group sets you apart from your peers. Can you hold a group's attention and call them to action in an entertaining way?

During this pizza session[19], Mark Robinson - and a special guest[20] - will show you:

- why so many presentations are mind-numbingly boring
- simple tricks to keep a group's attention
- how to use your presentation to create change

An hour after the email went out, I got a call from our Office Manager, Roxanne, who had

---

[19] TMC has *"pizza sessions"*: knowledge sharing evening meetings for its staff which start with pizza!

[20] Creating interest by adding a mystery... more on mystery later in this book. (Do you see what I did there?)

sent it. *"Mark, what have you done?"* I suddenly became anxious, "What's happened, Rox?"

She said, *"Within the first five minutes, 14 people signed up! And now you have 60 signed up, the room is full!"*

We had to turn people away. Apparently, I'd stumbled on a need felt by many people: the need to present confidently and professionally in front of a group.

But who was the *"special guest"* referred to in the email? That was my wife, Annelies. For her, presentations are a completely different experience than for me. She is one of the very few *natural* presenters, one from that small group of exceptions referred to in the previous chapter. She *looks forward* to speaking in front of groups! She *feels excited* when she has to give a presentation! Weird, right?

Before we go any further, I need you to do something. Watch my TEDx talk, or at least, the first three and a half minutes. Why? Because this introduction is very similar to the intro I gave at that workshop at TMC. It's the idea I had that day at the ASML reception.

If you keep going without watching it, you are about to hit a major spoiler. You've been warned! So watch this now:

> *How to present to keep your audience's attention* Mark Robinson; TEDxEindhoven
>
> https://youtu.be/BmEiZadVNWY

Done that? OK.

That introduction was remarkable on *that day* because it happened to be on the 50th anniversary of Dr Martin Luther King Jr's (MLK) *I Have A Dream* speech! So I started slightly differently. *"Imagine: it is exactly 50 years ago..."*

And I ended differently as well. After the MLK intro, I said, *"And now I'd like to introduce our special guest. She is here tonight to answer your presentation skills questions. A natural presenter who is, as of tomorrow, my wife of 15 years, please welcome: 'Annelies Robinson'!"* And with an introduction like that, of course she walked on to applause!

I need to prepare and practice all my speeches and presentations. Annelies just stood at the front and asked and answered questions spontaneously, with no preparation! And the evening was a huge success.

But I felt that the MLK introduction was special. There was more I could do with it. But what? And how could I inspire and help more people to develop their presentation skills?

I soon realised an opportunity would not land in my lap... I would have to create it! But how? And where would I find my audience?

How to start: get and keep their attention

"Oratory should raise your heart rate. Oratory should blow the doors off the place."
Rob Lowe as Sam Seaborn - character on The West Wing

What's a great way to *start* your presentation? How can some presenters grab your attention from the first words they speak? Why are you so interested right from the start?

Hello, my name is Mark Robinson and in this chapter, I will show you how to make the start of your presentations more clear, more focused and much more attention-grabbing.

So, how's that for a chapter opener? The format that I just used is the same format I teach people to begin their presentations.

There are three elements to it. Did you spot them?

In my workshop, there is one part that I find scary. I write, *"How to begin"* on a flip chart and then say, *"I will now show you how to begin a presentation. Would someone like to give me a topic?"* Then one person will shout a completely random topic and I immediately deliver the first 20 seconds of a presentation on that topic in a way that grabs everyone's attention. (On one occasion, one of the participants called out, *"Cows!"* as the random topic! This format still worked... but it was a tricky moment for me!)

Recently I asked a group to give me a topic and, after a moment's thought, one of the participants said, *"Climate Change".* So I said,

"Who here believes climate change is happening?[21] *Why is it happening? What can we do to prevent it? Good morning, my name is Mark Robinson and in the next 15 minutes I will show you what practical steps you can take today to ensure your children live happier, healthier and more ecologically friendly lives."*

Different topic, same structure. What is this structure? How does it work? And how can you apply it to your next presentation? I'm Mark Robinson and in this chapter, I will show you how applying this structure can make starting your presentations simple, quick and easy.

I did it again.

---

[21] At this point I get a show of hands. How I do that, without asking for it, will be explained later.

Before we examine the above structure (or template), let's agree on how *not* to start.

How not to start

"Light travels faster than sound. That's why certain people appear bright until you hear them speak."
Albert Einstein - Theoretical physicist

I was standing in front of 150 professional business people; the large screen behind me had just one word on it in large, black text on a bright white background: *"Presentations"*. The organisers had seen my TEDx talk and had asked me to give a five-minute talk, in Dutch, *"with a bit of British humour"*. The goal was to make a short advert for another presentation skills trainer who would be giving a workshop later that day.

I started with these words: *"Good morning everyone, first a bit about myself... I'm Mark Robinson. I'm 44 years old. I'm British. My hobbies are films, music and books. I'm married. We have two kids. And three rabbits named Huey, Duey and Nigel."*

As I said this, these words appeared in Dutch, one line at a time, on a slide behind me:

Introduction:

- Name: Mark Robinson
- Age: 44
- Nationality: British
- Hobbies: films, music and books
- Married
- Two children
- Three rabbits:
    - Huey
    - Duey
    - Nigel

The room was silent. These 150 professional, suited business people, including one famous Dutch politician, looked up at me with blank expressions. This was... not what I expected. Was my attempt at British humour not working?

I continued, the words I spoke now appeared *word for word* on the screen behind me:

Contents:

- Introduction (previous slide):
    - ○ Completely unimportant personal details about the speaker that no one is waiting to hear.

- Contents (this slide):
    - ○ The contents of the presentation: You know exactly what's coming and so decide:
        - ▪ *For the next hour, I'm just going to look at my smartphone*
    - ○ Told in so-called *"bullet points"*, because if he continues like this you will want to shoot the speaker.

- The rest of the presentation:
    - ○ *Is he now going to read every f***ing word of every f***ing slide to us?*

Then I stopped reading and turned, from the slides, to face the audience. Up to that point, I'd been using a monotone voice with my back to the audience. Now, in a more conversational tone, I said, *"OK, I've deliberately made several mistakes in this presentation. Can anyone tell me what they were?"* Silence. 150 pairs of eyes on me. Then, off the cuff, I said, *"Or is this normal at your company?"* Then they laughed. Yes, this was for them completely normal!

So many presenters, particularly at conferences, think that their first slide should be their CV and family situation. They will talk about the university they attended and show us pictures of the family, complete with Sebastian, the pet hamster. If you are tempted to do that, there is something you should know:

NO ONE CARES!

No one cares about your domestic situation. No one cares about your CV. And really no one cares about your hobbies[22]!

What do they care about? Themselves! Remember:

WII4ME

But after this spectacularly bad introduction, how do so many speakers compound their error? As I did, with the Table of Contents slide.

Never show a Table of Contents slide. Why? First, it's BORING. People will typically show this slide and then read it aloud to the audience! People's brains will start to switch off: if the presenter reads for you, you don't have to use your brain to read.

But most importantly, why spoil the mystery? Like the start of a good book, a great start of a presentation should intrigue people, give them hints as to what's coming without revealing it completely.

---

[22] I deliberately made mine vague (films, music and books) so that there would be absolutely no information contained in that part of the intro. It was pure hot air.

So, no CV and no Table of Contents. Is there any worse way to begin? Yes:

> **Presenter**, running on stage: *"OK, erm, how long do I have?"*
> **Organiser**, voice offstage: *"About 25 minutes"*
> **Presenter**: *"Really, only 25? I thought it was more like 2 hours. OK, let's get going and see how far I get. I'll go as fast as I can."*

At this point, the audience notices this in the bottom right corner of the first slide: "1/287"[23].

OK, so how should you then begin?

Let's reverse engineer the template at the start of this chapter. Then you will see how I can generate a *"catchy start"* in my workshop with no preparation. It's in three parts.

---

[23] Indicating the current slide number (1) and the total number of slides (287). This is going to be a looooooong 25 minutes.

Part 1: three questions

What is the *very first thing* every presenter needs to do? Answer: get your audience's attention. So how can you do that? There are many different ways. Some people begin with a joke. This can either be great... or terrible - it's a risk. Some people begin with a startling fact, *"PowerPoint is the primary cause of 86% of workplace fatalities!"[24]*

---

[24] Not really. At least, I don't think so. But why take the risk?

In my TEDx talk, I started with a mystery. I told people to, *"Imagine it's Wednesday 28 August 1963."* Of course, you are thinking, *"What happened on that date?"* And I've hooked you from the first sentence.

However, there is a much easier way: *ask questions.* Why is that? Because questions are a great way of getting people's attention. I pretend that inside people's heads are three switches. Normally these are all set to OFF. With each question, you flick one switch to ON. After three questions, they are completely focused on you and listening.

It's as if by asking questions you make space in people's minds, preparing them to receive the answers. So I also picture it as digging in the soil of your audience's minds, making a hole for you to plant new knowledge.

At this point in my workshop, I usually get asked, *"Do you have to* answer *these three questions in your presentation?"*

I reply that, for the purpose of getting attention, you can ask just about anything and, no, you don't even have to answer the questions in your presentation! So you could start by asking *"What day is it today? Why is the sky blue? If you were a tree, what kind of tree would you be and why?"*

And you would succeed in getting people's attention: the three switches would be flicked to ON.

However, I always ask questions related to my presentation: this is much more professional. And I always ask questions that I later answer during my presentation, just like I will answer the three questions at the start of this chapter. For me this is about integrity: if I asked questions I did not answer, I would feel that I am tricking my audience.

I'm also often asked, *"How can you generate those questions so fast?"* In my workshop, I do it on the spot. How do I do that?

Simple, I use the six W questions:

1. **W**ho?
2. **W**hy?
3. How**?** (This is the *"cheat"*W.)
4. **W**hat?
5. **W**here?
6. **W**hen?

And I tend to choose three *different* W words from the above list to start the questions. For example, I may choose, Who, Why and How, rather than three questions all starting with Why. This is so that I can think of different questions quickly.

In practice I tend to use only the first four: Who, Why, How and What. Why is that? These are the easiest to think up interesting questions:

- Who: this can become a poll question (a raise of hands).
- Why: this gets people thinking. It's the question humans ask naturally; ask any parent with kids under five...
- How: this is the clue to the WII4ME: if you can understand the *how,* you are a step closer to using this knowledge.

- What: this is one of the easiest to generate questions.

In case you are ever stuck for a question, here's one you can always ask as your third and final question: *"And why is this important for you?"*

So if *you* were asked to start a presentation on the topic of cows, you could start with, *"Who's ever seen a cow? What makes cows special amongst farm animals? And why is this important for you?"*

Part 2: greeting + name + X minutes

This is simple:

1. **greeting**: like *"Good Morning"*, *"Hello"*, *"Hi"* or *"Welcome"*
2. **name**: *"My name is <your name>"*
3. **X minutes**: *"and in the next <duration of presentation> minutes..."*

Why is this both necessary and powerful? First, this is a very short introduction to the speaker: it is *not* a long CV slide mentioning your love of goldfish. Believe me, people don't want to know more about you at the start than your name. They're waiting to hear the WII4ME and with this method, we get there as fast as possible.

Notice also that you mention how long your talk will take. This has a couple of benefits:

1. People know what to expect, which puts them at ease. Some level of ease is a good thing (but not a full table of contents which removes mystery).
2. People know you've prepared. If you say *"and in the next 30 minutes"* it conveys professionalism - you're ready for this talk. If you say, *"and in the next 28 minutes"*, they KNOW you've prepared and practiced!

If you do it right, you put it all together and get this:

"Good afternoon, my name is Mark Robinson and in the next 15 minutes..."

Why introduce yourself *after* the three questions? Because then you are sure people are listening. Starting with *"Good afternoon"* is what everyone does. That doesn't activate anyone's switches.

Tip: if your talk will be put online, avoid time-specific greetings like, *"Good morning"*, *"Good afternoon"* or *"Good evening"*. If people watch the video at a different time (or are viewing live in a different time zone), your talk will immediately start with a disconnect. Use *"Hello"* or *"Welcome"*.

Part 3: WII4ME

You've got their attention and introduced yourself. Next, you need to *keep* their attention. For that, you need to give them a reason to listen to the rest of your presentation.

To do this, you need to give them the WII4ME: What's In It For Me? Why should they listen to your talk? That's what they want to know and now, right at the start, you're going to tell them.

In sales training, you learn to speak about **benefits,** not features. For example, you don't say, *"This car comes complete with a state of the art flux capacitor"* when you could say, *"This car enables you to travel to any time, past or future."*[25]

This is why the *"Table of Contents"* start fails: it's all about the *features* of your talk. How instead can you focus on the *benefits*?

Here again, it is important to know your audience and their needs (see the previous chapter). Then you can tell them how your talk will benefit *them*.

The easiest way to do this is by using words that end in ER: richer, happier, healthier, faster, smarter, better, and so on. Or, when English does not permit this, use *"more <word>"*: more efficiently, more effectively, etc.

So you might end with, *"I will show you a way to complete your tasks faster, more effectively and with a higher return on investment"*.

----

[25] Assuming you are planning to sell a very special DeLorean.

Why does this approach work? First, because it makes people *want* to listen to the rest of your talk. They know What's In It For Them, and so they will pay attention (assuming you are telling them something they want to know). Secondly, did you notice how many benefits I listed? There were *three*. Three is a magic number, we'll talk more about that later. For now just remember: aim for the three benefits your presentation will give your audience.

Speaking of your audience, the main reason this approach works is this: your talk is *designed around your audience*. This start forces you to consider the benefits for your audience during your preparation. In other words, you are already focusing on what *they need to hear* rather than on what *you want to say*. It's a customer (audience) focused start.

When the people at my workshop hear this and then practice it (about midway through the morning), something shifts in the room. The realisation hits home, the penny drops: **the heart of your presentation is your audience's needs, not your content.**

What if you can't think of a benefit for your audience? Then either *you* can't think of it and you need help or there really is no benefit. If it's the former, go back to Ask The Audience. If it's the latter, why give a presentation at all?

With practice, you will think up some great benefits for your audience. From now on, your presentations will already get better because the needs of your audience will be at the centre.

But beware: when you first try this way of starting for yourself, it may feel unnatural. So keep practicing it - it will get easier and you will appreciate how much it benefits both you and your audience.

Part 4: a great way to continue

After the three benefits (WII4ME), you say, *"Let me tell you about something that happened to me two years ago that completely changed my life..."*

This is powerful for two reasons:

1. It's a direct command: *"let me..."*.
2. It's the start of a story.

We will address both these points later. For now remember: after your catchy start, launching into a *story* is a great way to follow. And this particular word choice is a powerful way because it refers to something in the recent past (*"two years ago"*[26]) and it was life-changing (because if it was *"life-changing"*, the audience knows something dramatic will follow and will be sitting on the edge of their seats).

---

[26] Longer than two years ago is *"distant past"* so less relevant; *"last week"* is unlikely to be *"life-changing"* - it hasn't passed the test of time yet.

Coming up...

You've made your start. You've got everyone in the audience looking up at you, hanging on your every word. Then what? How should you structure the rest of your presentation? In the next chapter, I will answer that by telling you the story of a very special French teacher.

Summary

A simple template to **start** is:

1. Three questions.
2. Greeting + name + x minutes.
3. WII4ME.
4. Tell a story (optional).

Exercise

Write down your catchy start to your presentation. See for yourself how it forces you to put your audience, not your knowledge, at the centre.

Three questions:

1.
2.
3.

Greeting + name + X minutes:

WII4ME (Benefits)

1.
2.
3.

" A presentation at ASML

"The harder I work, the luckier I get."
Samuel Goldwyn - film producer

There is an expression I love: *you make your own luck!* In other words, opportunities don't often come naturally, you have to create them.

But how could I apply that principle? I wanted to help my colleagues present better and I had this fun Martin Luther King Jr's intro. So what was the next step? I thought about this on and off for almost two years. Then I had an idea.

I contacted Daphne, the personal assistant of our department director at ASML. Could she arrange 15 minutes for me at the next department meeting?

So, in the autumn of 2015, I gave a talk to about 70 technical staff about presentations in ASML's auditorium. I began with my destruction of MLK's great speech with

PowerPoint and then went on to explain how you *should* present. This was the very first version of what would later become my TEDx talk.

It was a hit! They loved it. But I still felt there was more I could do with this talk. I just had to think bigger...

A simple yet powerful structure that works for any presentation

"Presentation is the 'Killer Skill' we take into the real world. It's almost an unfair advantage."
"The McKinsey Mind" by Ethan Rasiel & Paul N. Friga

The French teacher

Last year I went to a parents' evening at my daughter's new high school. About half a dozen teachers gave presentations to the 150 or so parents in the hall. To my surprise, all the presentations were instantly forgettable. For the most part, the teachers just read their PowerPoint slides to us.

All, that is, except one: the French teacher.

When she stood up to speak, the first thing she did was move the microphone stand from where it was (directly in front of the lectern) forward a couple of paces towards the audience. So when she spoke, it was not behind the lectern but in front of it, nearer to us. She had nowhere to store her notes because... she had no notes. And no PowerPoint.

Having taken a few moments to get everything as she wanted it, she explained that she needed the extra space because of her gestures. What was she planning?

She started by explaining that here (in The Netherlands) children learn to speak English easily because it's everywhere: in songs, on TV, on mobiles, computers, etc. But French is not, so it is much harder to pick up. And the traditional way of teaching French offers a very low return on investment: you have to put in a lot of effort and don't see immediate benefits, compared to English.

That traditional method is to have children learn French by *reading* it from a textbook and learning lists of vocabulary. This, she said, is quite different to how small children learn their first language: they learn it from *speaking* and using *gestures*.

So she said that in her French lessons the children speak only French and use gestures to communicate. Reading and writing only follow later (like a child's natural development). She demonstrated by drawing her hands down her body in a wavy motion while smiling and said, *"une fille"* (a girl). Then she put on a "cool" expression and raised her fists: *"un garçon"* (a boy)[27].

---

[27] It's hard to convey the power of this via text but it really worked for those of us in the room.

She then had all 150 of us parents repeat these gestures! This was why I remembered the gestures: it was another STAR moment. She also told us what the children thought of these lessons: they *love* this style. In her class the children move the tables and chairs to the side of the room so that they can move about easily to do these gestures. On one occasion she was late for a lesson. When she got to the room, the children had already moved the tables and chairs to the side of the class - they wanted to start as quickly as possible! How many school lessons are like that?

During her talk, there were two rounds of applause and a huge round of applause at the end. This was in complete contrast to the other presentations! What made her talk so powerful?

She used professional speaker techniques, like storytelling, direct commands, a natural enthusiasm and humour which made her talk very easy to listen to. I was amazed when I saw all this. It was like she had attended my workshop!

But she also used a very clear structure. Did you spot what it was? (If you've seen my TEDx talk, you may already recognise it.)

Let's reverse engineer this. You will see a simple structure which you can use in every presentation you give. If you use it, the structure will not only make your preparation much easier, but it will also make your presentations easier to follow and much more persuasive.

What is the Problem?

She started by highlighting the problem. English is everywhere in The Netherlands and is considered the *"world language"*. But French is not so common. Children don't hear it much and don't see the point of learning it. So they have a lot of resistance to learning French.

If, after your catchy start (see the previous chapter), you continue with the *problem*, you will immediately hook your audience. You have given your audience a puzzle and they will be thinking, *"how can this be solved?"*

They will also be wondering what solution you are proposing. So you will already be setting them up for *your* goal, what you want them to DO, to support or implement your solution.

But let's not get ahead of ourselves; let's first complete our analysis of the structure.

What is the Cause?

Why don't children learn French so well at school? The return on their investment is so low. It's not taught in a fun or even natural way so children have to invest a lot of effort. And what do they get for that effort? They get to learn French, but what can they do with that? They don't run into it on a daily basis like they do with English (probably a maximum of once a year, on a family holiday). So why, they might think, put in the effort?[28]

As you explain the cause, you are leading the audience to your solution by explaining your thought process: you bridge the otherwise wide gap between Problem and Solution. It will make your solution more plausible and so will increase the chances of people responding to your call to action.

You can put this (and each of these steps) into the form of a question, eg "Why don't children want to learn French?" We'll talk more about questions later. And you can add stories to each step (again, more later).

What are the Possible Solutions?

The teacher explained how this is usually solved in schools: children *read* textbooks and memorise lists of vocabulary.

---

[28] As a native English speaker who has learnt another language (Dutch), I can answer this. It broadens your horizons by giving you new ways to think. It does this by increasing your vocabulary (you will find words you simply cannot translate) and you will learn about a new culture which will also challenge many things you take for granted. So if you ever get the opportunity to learn a new language, do it!

She rejected this method because it is completely different to how children learn a language naturally.

If you include this step in your presentation, you can take the audience through solutions that they may already be considering. This enables you to anticipate and already handle many possible objections to your chosen or recommended solution.

What is the Chosen or Recommended Solution?

Her chosen solution was to teach the class in the same way children naturally learn! She speaks only French in her class and explains the words with gestures. And she was demonstrating that live in front of us (*"une fille", "un garçon"*) and even getting us to do it!

This is the moment you've been building up to and they've been waiting for: if you have prepared well, the **Chosen Solution** or **Recommended Solution** will be received with open arms. The problem is solved, the puzzle has its solution, the mystery is answered. The audience experiences closure and is ready for you to tell them what to do (that's in the next chapter).

By the way, the *chosen* solution is for when you're telling people how it is - they don't have any say in it. The *recommended* solution is when you are pitching to a decision-maker.

How will your solution benefit your audience?

When we discussed the *start* of your presentation, I stressed the need to get to the *benefits* of your talk. This is at the heart of all good sales techniques. What separates good salespeople from bad ones?

Here's the main difference: a poor salesperson will focus on *features*. *"Our laptops all have SSD drives."* A good salesperson will focus on the *benefits*. *"Because all our laptops have the new SSD drives, they start much faster, in just a few seconds."*

Think about how the French teacher did this: she didn't only tell us the *features* of her lessons (gestures, only speaking French) and stop there. No, she went on to talk about the *benefits*, for example that the students really enjoy the lessons and are motivated.

So when you talk about your Chosen (or Recommended) Solution, remember to explain how it will benefit your audience: translate the *features* of your solution to direct *benefits*. In other words, how will your solution make the lives of your audience members better? Or better still: WII4ME?

But I don't have a Problem!

Occasionally I hear this objection: *"My presentation doesn't fit this format because I don't have a problem to solve!"*

There are two possible answers:

- 99% of the time, there *is* a problem. The presenter just hasn't realised this yet.
- For the final 1%, there really is not a problem. But then, there is nothing worth presenting. Just send an email: *"Dear all, everything is OK. So I've cancelled my presentation."* You will be surprised at just how well your colleagues cope with this devastating news.

Shorter version

Are all four steps necessary?

Depending on your audience, you can ignore either the Cause or the Possible Solutions steps. Or both: you can jump straight from the Problem to the Solution. Usually, I think this is not better because people will only be sold on the solution if they can follow your thought process, as explained by the analysis (cause) and consideration of options (possible solutions).

But if these parts are obvious, feel free to skip them, especially if you have limited time (for example, when you are giving a two minute pitch).

Coming up...

And there you have it. This format gives you a focused, powerful presentation which will set you up for the end of your presentation. But how do you have a great ending to your presentation? That's coming up in the next chapter.

Summary

1. Use the format: Problem, Cause, Possible Solutions and Chosen (or Recommended) Solution.
2. In this format, each of these four sections can start with a question e.g. for Problem: *"Why don't our school children want to learn French?"*
3. If you have limited time, don't use all these steps. But always use the Problem and then Solution.

Exercise

For your presentation, get clear: what is the Problem you want to solve? What is the Cause? What are the Possible Solutions? Which have you considered? Which have you rejected? What is your Chosen (or Recommended) Solution and why?

For each step, consider what stories you can tell.

The **Problem** my presentation addresses is:

Here is a story about the problem (how I discovered the problem, what happened when the problem occurred or the consequences of the problem, ...)

The **Cause** of the problem is:

Here is my story of investigating that problem, how I got to the root cause.

Some **Possible Solutions** to the problem are:

Here are one or more stories of implementing those solutions. (Some might be successful, some might be failures - audiences are interested in both.)

The **Chosen** (or **Recommended**) **Solution** is:

Here is the story of trying out that solution, or how a similar solution worked elsewhere.

"

Filling the auditorium and turning more away!

"Find your voice and inspire others to find theirs."
Stephen Covey - author & speaker

I'd given a successful presentation in ASML's 150 seat auditorium but it was a small one: the auditorium was only half full. I had made my own luck when I arranged to speak at that department meeting; now the question was, how could I make *more* luck?

I approached InterCom (Internal Communication) at ASML and got into a conversation with Jens. He and I chatted over the possibilities and then we had an idea, which resulted in the following message being displayed on the ASML information screens throughout the main buildings:

Title: Presenting - How to keep your audience's attention?

Location: Auditorium

Start Time: 22 March 2016 11:30 AM
End Time: 22 March 2016 12:00 PM

Description: Mark Robinson shares his insights on why we keep losing our audience's attention and offers practical tips to make you a better presenter.

No registration required; first come, first served. Doors open at 11.15 AM.

I went early that morning to the auditorium. On the stage, I again went through my presentation to the empty room, as I had several times in the days leading up to this. Then I put on my headphones and began listening to energetic music (*Firestarter* by The Prodigy) to fire me up!

As I was listening to this, at about 11:00 someone came in. I stopped my energetic pacing on the stage, paused the music and said, *"Can I help you?"*

"Is this where the presentation skills talk is?"

he asked. *"Yes"*, I replied, *"But not for another half hour!" "That's OK, he said, I'll just sit here and wait."*

I'd never known anyone turn up early for a meeting at ASML, and here he was *30 minutes early!* A few minutes later, another turned up, and then another. At 11:20 - 10 minutes early - the auditorium was half full. What was happening? What had we started?!

Jens and I had decided to make it a, *"show up without a reservation"* event so we had no idea how many people would be present, or even if it would be a success at all. He'd publicised it via the internal channels but only for a week or so.

And yet, before 11:30 am, the auditorium was full. Then, due to fire regulations, they had to turn people away. The first to be turned away was one of my colleagues in my team who told me that he had arrived early to get a place!

He was the first of *many* to be denied access: *huge numbers of people were interested in developing their presentation skills!*

So I gave my prepared speech, with the MLK intro, and took some questions after. Jens had kindly arranged for the session to be recorded and said I could make the video publically available. You can watch it on my

YouTube channel[29]: *Presentation skills - how to keep your audience's attention*[30].

And the result? ASML was very happy with it and wrote an online article about my presentation[31].

So here was a *software consultant* speaking to 150 ASML-ers in a talk that got recorded and put online via official ASML communications!

My TMC account manager, Benjamin, commented at this point, *"Wow Mark, it can't get any crazier than this!"*

But he was wrong. It was about to get a lot crazier.

99

---

[29] https://www.youtube.com/c/markrobinsontraining
[30] https://youtu.be/jORl4e8pBil *"Presentation skills - how to keep your audience's attention (Mark Robinson at ASML)"* (Mark Robinson Training)
[31] https://medium.com/@ASMLcompany/martin-luther-king-did-not-use-powerpoint-and-neither-should-you-edb894bf5373

How to end: launch them into action!

"My job is to talk; your job is to listen. If you finish first, please let me know."
Harry Hershfield - cartoonist & author

How should you end your presentation? Why is this moment *critical* to achieving your goal? What do you need to say to get your audience into action?

The perfect end of your presentation consists of three parts. Before following the parts here, you will need to make sure that your goal is crystal clear. So if it is not, go back and reread the goal chapter. Ensure you know your **three main points** and your **call to action**.

The Perfect End, PE, is:

$$PE = 3MP + C2A + TQ$$

You can tell I'm an engineer, can't you?

3MP

3MP means your Three Main Points which we established in the goal chapter. These are the points that your audience *must* remember.

So you simply need to restate the three points. Don't forget: imagine that I will be outside the room and will ask everyone who leaves the same question, *"What was that presentation about?"* By restating these three points, no one will be left in any doubt what your main *"takeaways"* are.

You may also want to precede this by restating the problem you wanted to solve. Putting that all together (problem + 3MP):

"So how can we make presentations more interesting? By:

> 1. *having a clear goal,*
> 2. *using stories to keep an audience's attention and*
> 3. *ending with a call to action."*

Note how the problem is again stated as a question.

Tip: you can even count them off on your fingers to emphasise the three points.

C2A

Napoleon Hill - author (quote from *"Think and Grow Rich"*)

This is the moment you've been building up to, the C2A or Call To Action! This is where you finally speak out your **goal**: what you want people to **DO** as a result of your presentation. So tell them *as clearly as you can* what you want them to do.

We have defined this as part of our goal during our preparation: what do you want people to do after they leave the room?

Warning! There is a risk that you destroy your message here with a poor choice of words. So don't say, *"I hope you're going to..."* Don't ever *"hope"* anything at this point. Why not? Because you are making your message small. This is the moment where your message needs to be BIG! There will be more on removing *"dead phrases"*, later. For now, remember - don't say any of these:

- *"You now have enough information to..."*
- *"Have a think about doing..."*
- *"I hope you have enough information to think about doing..."* By the time you finally get to your C2A, the audience will have checked out!

So to be clear: this is the moment where YOU, and your message, need to be

BIG!

This is where you command your audience to take an action that will change their lives for the better. Did you get all that? You will:

- **command** your audience to
- **take** an action that will
- **change** their lives
- for the better (WII4ME)

Think: verbs, verbs, verbs. Verbs are *doing words*. It's a call to *action* not a call to *consideration*.

So tell them straight what you want them to do: give them a command. Your audience will appreciate your clear message.

You should always give a call to action. But when is that especially important? The answer is: during a *crisis*. The worst thing you can do in a crisis presentation, having whipped up the emotions with powerful stories of doom and gloom, is to end with, *"So sit tight, we're working on it!"* Your audience will think, *"NOOOOooooo! Give us something to DO to help fix this!"* Always give people something to do in a crisis.

C2As in real life

Goal	What you say	Why it works
An engineer wants programmers to test their work via a new tool.	*"From now on, make sure that all your code is fully tested using our new test suite."*	It's a clear instruction which also specifies when: *from now on.*
A promoter of a service or product wants people to start buying via a website.	*"So sign up today via my website to get a 20% discount!"*	This is also clear and it specifies when. In addition, saying, *"Today"* gives them a sense of urgency. If you can get people to respond the same day, the chance that they will obey your call to action is much higher! (It's also related to the Scarcity Principle[32]: what do you *feel* when you see, *"Hurry, while stocks last!"*?) And there is a clear WII4ME added to the C2A (the 20% discount). This increases the chance of acceptance even more.

---

[32] For more on the Scarcity Principle, see *Influence: Science and Practice* by Dr Robert Cialdini.

Goal	What you say	Why it works
A manager leading a reorganisation wants to make it a success by asking employees to bring a positive attitude to the changes.	*"Work with us during this reorganisation. Please come to us with any questions or concerns you may have. Bring the same positive, constructive attitude to this change that you bring to your day-to-day work. Let's make this a success together."*	Work, come, bring, make, ... four sentences, four verbs: each a C2A. And another persuasion technique: assuming they are already positive and constructive (third sentence). Inviting objections (*"Please come to us with any questions or concerns"*) lowers the chance of any offline complaining. Using a word like, *"Let's"* implies *"we are in this together"*.
A public speaker, who has spoken on the power of positive feedback, wants to create a more positive world and leave people with a positive impression of the speaker.	*"For the next week, only give positive feedback to everyone you meet: to your friends, to your colleagues and to your family. And see for yourself what effect positivity has on your life."*	Again, it's a clear message and it specifies *when*. And it's a positive message which leaves your audience with a great feeling when your talk is finished. (This is a real call to action I use when I give speeches about the power of positive feedback.)

TQ

You should end by saying *"thank you"*[33]. This is the universal way of signalling to your audience that your speech has finished.

But wait: this is a crucial moment, your *final second*! This determines the *feeling* people have when they leave the room. We'll look at this in the next chapter. Before that, one crucial tip, which is powerful, easy to implement but so easily forgotten.

---

[33] For those unfamiliar with this uncommon abbreviation (TQ), *"thank you"* sounds like *"thank queue"*.

117

Series of presentations

Let's say you are going to give a *series* of presentations, one after another. These might be multiple workshops on one day, a regular talk at work or even a weekly sermon. How can you end in a way that makes people want to attend the next talk?

The answer is: you ask them *questions* which you will only answer in your next talk. For example, let's say you are giving a series of talks on *"team communication"*. At the very end, just before the TQ, you ask:

- *"What are the major challenges in team communication?"*
- *"Why do teams like ours in all companies have so many communication failures?"*
- *"And how can we encourage great communication in our daily work?"*

Notice I ask three questions. Does that seem familiar? We did exactly this with our catchy start. So these three questions form the end of one presentation and can be used as the *start* of the next!

And don't forget to add this call to action: *"Join us for the next talk!"* Then you end with, *"Thank you"*.

I use this technique in my workshops. When we have a break I say something like, *"What should you do if you feel nervous? Can we use our nervousness as a positive force? And how can a glass of water help us? The answer is coming up after the break!"*

I also use this in every content chapter in this book. Speaking of which...

Coming up...

So, what should you do in your final second on stage? Do you just say, *"thank you"* or is there more to it? The answer is coming up!

Summary

PE = 3MP + C2A + TQ

The Perfect End (PE) is:

1. 3MP: recap the three main points people *must* remember.
2. C2A: *tell them* what to **do**; do not ask or *"hope"*.
3. TQ: say *"thank you"* (see next chapter).

Does this look familiar? I end all my chapters with 3MP + C2A!

Exercise

Your end, especially your call to action, must be confident! Write down your ending and then practice it.

You do not have to memorise every single word. You're speaking from the heart, not from memory. But by writing it down first you are able to get a draft plan for your ending.

Here are the three things I want my audience to remember, written as I will state them in my presentation:

       1.

       2.

       3.

       My call to action to the audience, written as I will state it, is:

After writing it down here, practice your ending out loud, either on your own or to a trusted audience (family members or colleagues). Do this at least 10 times or until you can deliver it with confidence.

Pitching for TEDx

"That looks like a TED talk!"

Martin, one of my friends, made that comment after watching the ASML video. I'd heard of TED[34] talks: popular presentations on a variety of topics delivered by professional presenters within a time limit of 18 minutes. I'd also heard how TED was creating local versions all across the world, called TEDx[35]. Giving a speech at one of these venues is very rare and quite an honour.

Undaunted, I typed *"TEDx Eindhoven"* into Google. I found out that there was a TEDx in Eindhoven and that it was going to have its first conference in a few months. I also saw that there was a pitch event in a few weeks and that the closing date for submissions was

---

[34] https://www.ted.com
[35] https://www.tedx.com

in a couple of days! What a coincidence, what an opportunity!

People often ask me, *'How can I become a TEDx speaker?'* There are exactly two ways that I know of:

- get invited, because you've done something amazing or
- win a pitch event.

I hadn't done anything amazing enough to be *"TEDx worthy"*. But I did have an important message. So, I decided to give the pitch event a shot and submitted my written talk summary, or *"abstract"*, with a link to the ASML talk.

Then I waited. A few days later, this arrived in my inbox:

An email with good news!

We have chosen you to pitch on the TEDx stage! TEDxEindhoven has formed a super team of speakers with various backgrounds. We are very happy with the result!

I was invited to pitch!

The date was a problem: Sunday 15 May 2016 was in the middle of our family holiday. We had booked a long weekend away at a nearby holiday park. However, my wife agreed this was too good a chance to miss.

So on Sunday afternoon in the middle of our mini-holiday, I was in the swimming pool with my daughters, thinking *'In just a few hours I will be giving my TEDx pitch!'*

I spent a lot of time on both the Saturday and the Sunday morning practicing my pitch out loud, as I had in the run-up to the weekend. The pitch was to last a maximum of six minutes. So I timed my practices and killed my darlings, all to make sure it fit in that short time.

At about 5 pm, I kissed my family goodbye, left the holiday park and drove to Eindhoven. TEDxEindhoven had hired the top floor of a building called the *"Het Ketelhuis"* (translated: The Boiler House) in Eindhoven, a large room which seated about 200 people.

As I nervously waited, I watched several people give very high-quality pitches. I seriously wondered if I would have *any* chance of being chosen.

I was one of the last of the 13 people invited to pitch that evening (of the many, many written applications the organisers had received). After the host introduced me, I walked up onto the stage and turned to face my crowd.

You can watch my pitch on YouTube[36]. If you do, you will hear bottles crashing together during my speech. The room had a bar, the contents of which help those present to appreciate my British sense of humour. They even laughed on one occasion when I didn't intend a joke!

Here's how that happened: many of the other speakers used their six minutes to give mini versions of their full talk. I had a different strategy. During the preparation, I thought, *"This is a pitch event, you don't reveal your whole talk, right? You just give a teaser."*

So instead, after my MLK intro, I said, *"Here's my pitch: if my talk is chosen, I'll share with you the two best techniques that I know for speaking in front of a group."* This was the cause of the unintended laughter. Whereas many of the others gave away their full speech content for free, I kept secret my *"two best techniques"*. This, I hoped, would give

---

[36] https://youtu.be/0J9V7uc1CJw *"TEDxEindhoven pitch Mark Robinson May 2016"* (Mark Robinson Training)

them an added reason to pick me.

And then, after chatting with and thanking a few of the organisers, I left to resume my family holiday and await the result.

What should you do in the final second?

"The energy level of the audience is the same as the speaker's. For better...or for worse."
Andras Baneth - author & speaker

Why is the final second important?

You've given your talk, it's been amazing. You've caught their attention from your first words. You've got a logical structure, starting with a problem your audience recognises and feels. You end with a solution with which they agree. You've kept their attention with questions, stories and STAR moments. And then you end with your call to action: a smart implementation of your proposed solution. The room is buzzing with energy.

And then... then the room goes...

... silent?

Nothing.

That's it?

You feel it in the air... they want to applaud, but don't.

Instead, they quietly file out of the room. The energy you created has drained away. The moment lost. And it all hinged on the final second.

Afterwards, a couple of people come up to you and say the same thing.

"That was so good, I wanted to applaud, but no one else did."

This is what you **must** avoid. It's a lose / lose; for you and your audience. They go from feeling great to feeling... *meh!*

How can you prevent this? Before I answer that, how should you not end?

How not to end your presentation

I've seen terrible endings of presentations. Here are some ways *not* to end, together with the reasons why:

- *"OK, I think that's all I wanted to say."* Energy level: zero.
- *"To be honest, I didn't prepare so well, I just made it up on the spot."* Translation: *"It was pretty bad, wasn't it?"*
- *"Oops, did I run over time?"* We saw in the chapter on preparation, always check in advance how long your presentation should last. Practice speaking within that time and when you go live - stick to it!

So, how should you end?

The answer is surprisingly simple. You need to do four things in one second, The Final Second.

Before I tell you what they are, let's consider: why is it important to get applause?

If you get applause, the people will feel that exhalation. You've built them up to it; let them exhale.

And... (here comes the sneaky part) it makes your message more persuasive.

Think about it! If people applaud you, they are much more likely to do what you told them (in the call to action). Why? Because people *have a need to be consistent!*[37] So after showing that they love your talk by giving you enthusiastic applause, they will continue to love your message long after you've given it.

---

[37] For more on our need for consistency, see *Influence: Science and Practice* by Dr Robert Cialdini.

The four steps to unleash applause

I say *"unleash"* here because you don't get applause for free, not even if you do these four things. You've got to *earn* it. You build it up by applying all the techniques in this book. When you've done that, do these four simple things all in that final second - and then they *will* applaud.

Those steps are:

1. Say, *"Thank you"*. You can otherwise say something similar, *"Thank you for listening"* or *"Ladies and Gentlemen, thank you very much for your attention"*. The point is that you *thank* your audience.
2. Take a little bow.
3. Clap your hands together once.
4. Take a step back. And in that vacuum you create, in the space in front of you and in the time when you go silent, they will applaud.

Want to see that? Check out my TEDx talk. There it happens twice!

Which of these is obligatory? The answer is, the first. Your final sentence must be to thank the audience. Then everyone knows your talk is finished.

Coming up...

So now the structure of your talk is clear, from catchy start to the final second. How can you keep your audience listening with anticipation, sitting on the edge of their seats, hanging on your every word? The answer is in our next chapter but here's a clue: I'm using that trick right now, did you spot it?

Summary

1. Aim for applause, it's a win for you and your audience.
2. Thank you, bow, clap once, step back. All in one second.
3. Saying *"thank you"* is a must, to be polite and to show that the presentation has ended.

Exercise

Draw ten boxes in two columns on a piece of paper.

☐	☐
☐	☐
☐	☐
☐	☐
☐	☐

Practice the "four steps in one second" ending five times, using the check boxes in the left column to track your progress.

Then imagine you have just ended your presentation which went fantastically well. Do these four steps again and then imagine your audience bursting into applause. Again, do this five times, checking the boxes in the right column.

Not only will this give you a flawless ending, but you will also be training yourself to expect success.

Whenever you practice a presentation, ensure you also practice The Final Second.

Am I dreaming?

"Big results require big ambitions."
Heraclitus - philosopher

The result of the pitch was due the next day, on the Monday. Would I be one of the lucky ones from that group of 13? I doubted it. There were many people with interesting topics who could present well. Why would they pick me?

Monday was also the last day of our family holiday. I tried to enjoy it as best as I could and especially to be there for our two girls. But my mind was often elsewhere. At any moment I would get an answer from TEDx.

Or so I thought. Instead, I got a message that day to say that the result was delayed, it was now expected on Tuesday. Even longer to wait! I was like a little child waiting for Christmas Day - would I get what I was hoping for?

On Tuesday I went back to work at Eindhoven's High Tech Campus, a business park for many high-tech companies.

Throughout the morning I did my best to concentrate on my work, but it was not easy.

Then, on Tuesday 17 May 2016 at 12:10 pm, I received an email from TEDxEindhoven. Here's part of it (translated from Dutch):

Dear Mark,

We discussed all the pitches with the jury and selected three winners.

One of these is you!

I was in! It was so unreal... was I dreaming?

And then I realised... it was scheduled for 8 July: we would go live in less than two months! Was that enough time? What would I need to do beforehand? How should I prepare to speak on a *fricking TEDx stage?!*

What was that about questions?

"Judge a man by his questions rather than by his answers."
Voltaire - author & philosopher

Why are questions so powerful?

There - did you feel it?

'Feel what?' you think. That's the power of questions. I've got you now. You want to keep reading until you find the answer.

And the longer I leave it, the more annoying the feeling, right?

That's why questions are so powerful: they create a mystery that *must be answered*. They are only half of a whole: you must discover the answer to complete the puzzle. Until then, what do you *feel*? Some discomfort? Intrigue? Tension?

Whatever you feel, now you know the power of questions. And as a presenter, wanting to keep your audience's attention, this knowledge is priceless. And it will also help *you* when you prepare and structure your presentation. But we'll come to that in a moment.

First: what are the three powerful question types available to presenters? (And there's another question: this technique is useful for presenters and authors!)

Normal sentence?

The first type is when you turn a normal sentence into a question. That's easy, right? You just say a normal sentence but end it with a question, don't you? And *you* could do that, couldn't you? You've seen what I'm doing, yes? It's not difficult, is it? But it does funny things to your brain, doesn't it?

OK, enough. You get the point. By adding just a couple of words to the end of a sentence, you can make it into a question. And simply by doing this, you *will* get attention.

These questions are not meant to be answered. They are simply there to reset people's attention span. So don't machine-gun them out at your audience, as I did to you in the first paragraph. But use them from time to time, particularly if you notice attention dropping.

Now, from a question that is *not* meant to be answered to one that *must* be...

How can I introduce the next topic?

The second type is when you use a question to kick off a topic. By this I mean you ask a question and *then answer it yourself.* How would that look? (Do you see what I did there?)

Let's take an example of a presentation structure where we see only the questions:

- What's happening with sales at our company?
- Why is this happening?
- What should we make of this?
- Why is this bad news?
- What is the management team doing to improve sales?
- What do we want you to do?

What do you notice about this? There are three lessons for us in this list of questions.

First, by using this structure you will get and keep attention. With each question, you will keep people's attention until they hear the answer. And then when you ask the next question, you reset their attention span. It's like magic!

Consider for a moment the alternative. Here is *exactly* the same content, but in the standard, non-question, format:

- Company X sales, Q3, 2020
- Sales analysis
- Response to sales analysis by management team part 1 / 2
- Response to sales analysis by management team part 2 / 2
- Action plan of the management team
- Company impact

It's *so dull*, isn't it? Did you feel your eyes get heavy as you read the list? Or did you just skip the list? Here's the secret:

The *content* is the same; it's all in the **presentation!**

Secondly, from the list of questions you already have a great idea of what the presentation is about, much better than with the non-question list. For example, you know it is bad news and that you are part of the solution. Have you ever heard that presentation format tip: *"Tell them what you're going to tell them, tell them, tell them what you told them"*? If you practice this literally, it will be boring. But using this format you've already told them the main points twice: in the questions and in your answers. (And the third time will be in your ending, remember the 3MP?)

Speaking of *format*, did you spot it? Here's the third and final lesson: the format was: problem, cause and solution, the *"French teacher format"*.

Hands up those who think questions are an effective way to get attention?

Here is a really simple trick to reset the attention of *everyone* in the room: you simply ask for a show of hands. The only tricky part is choosing the right question.

There are two mistakes you could make here:

1. Asking a confusing question: *"Do we have a culture of clarity or don't we?"* Er... should I raise my hand? Instead, ask a *binary* question where Yes means raise your hand and No means don't raise your hand.
2. Asking a question where the majority response is No. I did this wrong once when I was giving a presentation skills workshop in the south of France. Normally the weather there is great but on this occasion, it was raining. I asked, *"Who likes this weather?"* One or two hands went up. What I should have asked is, *"Who prefers sunny weather?"*

So, you need to ask a *clear* question where the majority of people raise their hands. But wait, why do you want the majority of people to raise their hands? Two reasons:

1. You want maximum engagement. When people move, in this case by raising their hands, they are engaged. They are paying attention to what you say and responding.
2. You want *influence*. When you ask for, and get, a show of hands, you are starting to establish yourself as the *leader* of the group. As we will see later, you are training them to follow your commands. And this means they will be more ready to accept other commands you may give, including your Call To Action.

Now, I said, *"ask for... a show of hands"* but how do you do that? Here's where you can spot the difference between trained presenters (including you as a reader of this book) and all the others.

The others will say, *"Who here agrees it is important for a presenter to engage with their audience?* **Hands up!***"*

The trained presenters, and you after today, will never use that word combination. Instead, you will say, *"Who here agrees it is important for a presenter to engage with their audience?"* And then you will *raise one hand in the air.* You will also pause and look from one side of the audience to the other. You will not say, *"Hands up!"* like you are about to arrest them. By simply raising your hand others will follow your lead. Watch in amazement next time you do this!

You could even try this: Ask, *"How many people think I can influence you to move your body with a non-verbal gesture?"* Raise your hand. Look out onto a sea of raised hands... realise your power of influence...

Everyone in the room will increase their attention level when you ask for a show of hands. This includes even those who had started to fall asleep! At the very least, they will wake up, look around at the sea of raised hands and wonder what everyone else is doing. And then they might even raise *their* hand. No one wants to feel the odd one out, right?

Coming up...

These three types of questions are powerful ways to keep attention. What's coming next is an even more powerful method... and it's one you've known since you were a little child.

Summary

There are three types of questions a presenter can use to get attention:

1. Turn a normal sentence into a question. These aren't meant to be answered, are they?
2. Introduce a topic with a question. So that's two types... what's the third type?
3. Ask the audience for a show of hands. How many of you will try this during your next presentation?

Exercise

Plan your presentation in terms of the questions you will answer. What will the first one be? Answer: a variation on, *"What is the problem?"* If you use PowerPoint, you can even introduce each slide with a question.

You can also turn some of your sentences into questions (can't you?). And finally, add one question where you ask for a show of hands.

Here is the list of questions my presentation will answer:

1.
2.
3.
4.
5.

And here are a few normal sentences from my presentation, but rewritten into a question format:

1.
2.
3.
4.
5.

Here's at least one question I can ask to get a show of hands:

"

Preparing for TEDx

"One important key to success is self-confidence. An important key to self-confidence is preparation."
Arthur Ashe - professional tennis player

How many times do you think I practiced my TEDx talk? The answer is more than a hundred times! I had to get it right, not just for the 300 people in the room but also for the thousands who would watch it later online.

So over the next eight weeks, I was very busy. I practiced my talk almost every day. When I practice, I always practice *out loud*. If I practice in my head, the speech will sound great *in my head* but when I speak it out loud it all goes wrong.

So, I practiced out loud in my front room, in the shower and even as I cycled to work. Those 20 or so minutes daily cycling were an ideal time to practice... except that the people cycling in the opposite direction must have thought, *'Who's that crazy guy who is always muttering to himself?'*

I sometimes took an evening walk just so that I could practice my talk undisturbed (no doubt only enhancing my reputation as a muttering idiot). I practiced in front of my wife and in front of colleagues. I even practiced on the TEDx stage!

By a happy coincidence, the 2016 TEDxEindhoven conference was relocated to Eindhoven's High Tech Campus - which is where I was working. So during my lunch break or at the end of the day, I often went to the main *"Einstein"* auditorium, stood on the stage and delivered my speech to an empty hall. I imagined the audience, the lights and the cameras all focused on me. I was trying to acclimatise to the idea... but it was still a scary prospect.

Of course, the TEDx team gave their support to all of us speakers. We had a day of practicing our presentations together at the Eindhoven University of Technology (or TU/e), facilitated by Serge, a professional trainer. The tips I received from Serge, and from my fellow presenters, further helped to improve my speech. For example, I originally wrote on the flip chart in lower case letters. But my writing is illegible! So I was advised to write in capital letters - great advice!

We even got clothing tips. I felt very proud going to a clothing shop and saying, *"I need a jacket that can be seen well on camera!"*

And for the day itself, we all had to take a spare set of clothes. The last thing you want is to have your TEDx talk immortalised by a coffee stain on your shirt!

Meanwhile, my parents and brother were preparing to come over from England to watch the talk. My wife, father-in-law and Benjamin, my TMC account manager, had also got tickets. So I had my supporters - and I was beginning to get really nervous.

The evening before, we gathered at a restaurant in Eindhoven: the team, the speakers and the artists who would perform acts between the speeches. Because of my nervousness, I remember almost nothing of the evening, except thinking: this time tomorrow it will all be over... for better or for worse!

Once upon a time...

It was a cold winter morning in the courtyard. Armed soldiers stood around the perimeter, watching the drama unfold.

At one end stood a man holding a crossbow. He was a good man, a hero to the people in these parts. At the other end stood a frightened young boy, held between two guards. Another guard walked up to the boy and placed an apple into his shaking hands. "Hold this!" the man said, sternly. "No, boy, hold it on your head!"

The boy slowly lifted the apple to his head. The guard glared across the courtyard to the man with the crossbow and nodded. The man lifted his crossbow, looked down the arrow shaft at first the boy, his son, and then at the apple. Then he fired.

To understand how this brave hunter came to be firing

> *an arrow at his son, we need to wind the clock back a few hours, to the late afternoon of the previous day...*

Intriguing isn't it? A story is started, but not yet finished. Like a question without an answer, it hangs there, demanding your attention, and does not let go until it is ended. (And there we will leave this story. If you want to know how it ends, look up the story of William Tell.)

Why are stories so powerful? One word:

Mystery

You need to know *how the story ends*. And until then, just like with a question, you stay with it until the mystery is answered. The power of the story keeps you waiting faithfully till the end.

That's why so many of my chapters end with a question. I give you half of a whole and to get the other half you must read the next chapter. Or I might just drop a clue, as I did in the previous chapter when I said that *this* chapter would contain a method for keeping attention that you've known since you were a little child. If you have children, you'll know how much they'll demand a bedtime story. Everyone loves stories. So why not make use of that?

So stories *keep your attention*. But that's only a part of what makes them so powerful. Before I tell you the other reasons (did you see what I did there?), let's answer, *"What are the ingredients of a great story?"*

Ingredients

"Storytelling is about two things; it's about character and plot."
George Lucas - filmmaker

All stories contain two elements:

1. a **Person**: the main (or hero) character and
2. a **Problem** to be solved; this drives the plot.

That's normally it. But for our purpose, there is also a third element:

3. a **Point** or a reason for telling the story.

Let's look at these 3Ps one at a time.

Person

Stories are all about people. Our presentation stories will often be about one specific person. This is the central character or hero of the story. Who is the hero? Typically this will be you, as you talk about an experience that happened to you. Or maybe it is a colleague or family member, a famous person, a stranger or a fictional character.

The closer that person is to you, the better, because then you will convey the character's emotions. If you talk about a famous person who caught a bank robber, that has power. But if you talk about how your *mum* did that, that will have a bigger kick! (Yes, my Mum caught a bank robber. Now you want to hear the story, right? See how powerful stories are?)

But who is the *best* hero character? Let me ask it another way: who does *your audience* want the hero to be?

Pretend you are in my workshop as I tell the group the following story to introduce the topic: *"how to end your presentation"*:

Imagine you are coming to the end of a super important presentation. You've been planning this for weeks. You've got a clear goal. You've invested many hours in preparation, perhaps two hours for every minute of this presentation. You've had a great, catchy start. You've clearly explained the problem and the cause. You've dealt with several possible solutions and explained why they won't work. Then you've outlined your recommended solution.

You've even wowed them with a STAR moment: they are never going to forget this! And then you say,

"Um, I think that's all I wanted to say. I'll stop there..."

And then you shuffle offstage. With every step you take, the energy you've built up in the room dissipates. And what changes as a result of this presentation?

Absolutely nothing.

How can this be different? How should you end your presentation so that you achieve your goal, to ensure action?

Who is the hero? Your audience! Whenever you can, make *them* the main character of the story.

Does that sound familiar? Do you remember something similar from my TEDx talk? There I made the audience an active part of the story, right from the first few seconds.

Problem

We saw this in the *French teacher* chapter. Near the start of every *presentation*, you want to hook people with this question: what is the problem to be solved? In the same way, a story will start with a problem.

In The Netherlands, there is a huge amusement park called The Efteling. In the middle is the *"Fairytale Forest"* where children can visit magical locations and meet various characters. One of these is the Fairytale Tree. The children sit on benches in front of the tree and he opens his eyes and talks to them. He tells them fairy tales about all the characters in the Efteling.

What makes it special for us as presenters is how he *starts* these stories, which is always with exactly the same words. He says, *"In the Fairytale Forest we usually live long and happy lives. But there was once a day that that wasn't so..."*

So begins the problem, and hence the story. And it keeps our attention until the problem is solved, at the end of the story[38].

For our purposes though, the solution does not need to be *in* the story. In my TEDx talk, the story of my first presentation at school explained the problem: I had no idea how to give a presentation. This problem was raised in the story but not solved in it; that's what the rest of the TEDx talk is about.

So make sure you know what the problem is. Then you can decide to tell either a story which includes the solution or one that merely highlights the problem.

Point

Why are you telling the audience this story? It's got to be related to your message. In the story in the *"Person"* section above, the purpose was to introduce the topic, *"How to end your presentation"* in my workshop.

So the reason for telling a story can be to start a new subject. Or it can be to highlight a problem (as with The Empty Box story, later in this chapter). Or it can be to

---

[38] Notice how every story starts with a problem. Sometimes, when life throws me a tough time, I think, *"Well, at least I'll get a good story out of this."*

trigger your audience to think of the solution, as with the French Teacher story. So before you add a story, consider: why are you telling this? How does it relate to the goal of my presentation? If your story does not have a point relating to your goal, it's just another darling waiting to be killed.

Please bear in mind: you don't have to be Shakespeare! Nobody's going to give you professional literary criticism. You simply talk about an experience of yours, or someone else, in a way that has a clear message for us.

So now think about the story chapters in this book. Notice how they follow this 3P story format. There is a Person, or hero: me (yeah, that's a bit awkward). And there is a Problem: I hated public speaking because I sucked at it! Finally, there is a Point, they all reinforce the main message of this book: if *I* can, *you* can!

Timing

Stories in presentations are interesting! They will keep your audience's attention. But *only if* they are not too long. Remember the 3 Es? If you have too much Entertainment, people will think, *"where's the content (Education)?"* So aim for a story of about 15-30 seconds. It may be longer, but rarely will a presentation story be longer than one minute.

So cut out every detail of the story that does not drive the plot: *kill your darlings* also applies to storytelling!

Keep them in suspense

I first understood this technique when I read about it in a British newspaper article[39] by Charles Moore. (I read this seven years ago but still remember it - that's the power of stories!) It's a story of when Boris Johnson, who was then a humble MP, uses this technique in another newspaper article.

Johnson tells the story of when he was giving a political speech and one of his opponents, a Labour councillor (a political opponent), threw a bread roll at him, aiming for Johnson's head! But for the rest of the article, Johnson ignores it, *"leaving the roll in mid-air"* in the words of Moore. Johnson's article then covers all the things he wants to say, leaving the reader wondering what happened to the roll. Only at the end of his article is the suspense resolved: Johnson explains that the bread roll hit him full in the face.

I find it amazing how an act which could have been described as simply, *"He threw the roll at me and it hit me in the face,"* was instead used so effectively to keep the reader's attention.

I use this technique in this book: did you see when I used it in this chapter? It was in the William Tell story (though I did

---

[39] https://www.telegraph.co.uk/news/politics/9449612/Is-Boris-Johnson-serious-When-it-comes-to-No-10-the-answer-is-deadly-so.html

not resolve it). I also use this in the Daphne story which you will read later.

To summarise: you stop a story at the point where people think, *'What's going to happen?',* leaving the mystery temporarily unresolved. You can also take this one step further: leave them thinking, *'how will our hero(s) get out of this?'* This is how I started this book, right from the first paragraph I plunge the reader into a tense situation.

One level deeper: the A / B plot

One of my favourite TV shows from the 90s was *Star Trek: The Next Generation*. TNG (as us fans call it) was known for using the A / B plot trope, or plot + sub-plot approach.

The idea is simple: you start with plotline A then stop on a cliffhanger and start plotline B. You then stop B on a cliffhanger and jump back to A[40]. With this *simple* trick you keep people hooked! They are continually in suspense: at all times they are wanting to know how at least one of the plots will continue. (TV series go even further: they have a story arc over the whole series. For example, think about Star Trek: Voyager which had a plot over the whole seven seasons to return to Earth.)

---

[40] https://tvtropes.org/pmwiki/pmwiki.php/Main/TwoLinesNoWaiting

Do you see how I am using this technique in this book? I have two types of chapters:

- *training chapters*: where you learn my workshop content to improve your presentation skills and
- *story chapters*: where you read my story to inspire you

Both end in a way to make you want to read the next chapter of that type. But before that, you read the other chapter which also makes you want to keep reading! If you find this book hard to put down, this trick will have worked.

So this technique can be used in writing. But can it be used in a presentation? Yes, it can: I used it in my TEDx talk. Do you remember when?

I started with the Blackbird story, then stopped to tell the story of my daughter's presentation about England and then I went back to finish the Blackbird story. Interweaving two stories like this may be too much for many presentations. However you can certainly use the easier variant: start one story and leave it halfway through (continue with your presentation), only to complete it later.

Micro suspense

What if you have a moment in your story where you want people to give *extra* attention? This is likely the "pivot" moment, where your story moves from problem to solution. How do you get your audience to be extra alert at that crucial moment?

In the next minute, you will learn how to create a burst of suspense, so that everyone will be on the edge of their seats.

First, how is this different from what we just discussed? The way to keep them in suspense mentioned in the previous section, by pausing a story halfway, works over several minutes. They are hanging on every word waiting for you to complete the story.

What if you want to keep them in suspense but over a shorter interval? Specifically, how can you get your audience to give extra attention to what you say in the *next sentence* of your story?

I've used the technique just now: I asked you a question (we covered this in an earlier chapter). And the preceding paragraphs contain several questions, don't they?

Another way to get that "micro suspense" is to use an attention-grabbing phrase, like:

- *"And then, I had an idea."*
- *"What happened next would change everything."*
- *"Then came a moment that would change my whole life."*

And these examples are all used in this book:

- *"Before I tell you what they are"*
- *"It was about to get a lot crazier."*
- *"Or so I thought!"*
- *"What happened next was a masterclass in persuasion!"*

- *"In the next minute, you will learn..."* (Used just a few paragraphs before!)

Of course, you can only use these if they are *true*. It's not going to look good if you say, *"What happened next would change everything: Bob emailed me the sales projections and they were exactly what we expected."* No, use them before you introduce *drama* into your story! And do add drama - people want to *feel* your presentation at least as much as they want to *hear* and *see* it!

Why are stories so powerful?

Mystery

I already said that one reason stories are so powerful is, *"Mystery"*. That's what keeps your attention.

But there are more reasons.

Memorable

For a presentation to result in change, it must be *memorable*. People have to remember what they have to do (the call to action) and *why* they need to do it (one or more of the three memorable points).

But how can you make sure that people will remember what you've told them to do long after your presentation? Answer: use stories. Your audience will forget most of your presentation before they leave the room. But the *stories* will be remembered for a long time. Why is this? Someone once described a story as being like a robot that keeps working in your brain long after you've heard it.

For example, I once heard of an All Employee Meeting at a certain company where the CEO told the *"empty box story"*. A supplier had ordered an urgent spare part but what they received was... an empty box. I happened to know some of the employees who attended this meeting. They all remembered different details of the meeting but *all of them* remembered the *"empty box story"*.

Use a story to illustrate your point and people will listen *and remember* - and therefore *act.*

Speaking of action... *why* do we decide to act? What makes us decide on one particular course of action and reject another? As we will see later (when we discuss POTUS[41] 45), we rarely make decisions based on *facts.* More often, we decide with our *emotions* and afterwards, we rationalise the decision with our *brains.*

Can we, as presenters, make use of this?

---

[41] I use POTUS as an abbreviation for President of the United States throughout this book. This is to give extra highlight to the number of US presidents who have been such powerful orators.

Emotions

We are not talking to robots, Vulcans or even (for the most part) the British[42]. We are talking to humans just like us with broadly the same hopes and fears. So if you want to connect with your audience, speak not only to their head but also to their heart. How do you do that?

Tell them how you felt during your story. Or, if the story is not about you, you can tell them how you felt when you heard it. Use phrases like:

- *"We were all so excited when..."*
- *"I was devastated."*
- *"So imagine my feeling when..."* This last one is used in this book. It is especially powerful both because it is a direct command and because I don't tell you how I felt but you have to figure it out - which also keeps your attention. And even if what you imagine is different to the feeling I actually had, does it matter?

So if you use stories, you will keep your audience listening because of the mystery. And people will remember the stories and be emotionally moved by them. But so what? What is the ultimate goal of telling your audience stories?

---

[42] Self-deprecating humour is in our DNA.

Change

"Presentations are only as good as the change they bring about. Your presentation has no value unless it is acted upon."
Mark Robinson - software consultant, speaker & author

It's even worse than that quote above, presentations cost money - a lot of money. Let's assume you follow the one hour preparation for every one minute presenting rule. For a presentation of 30 minutes to 100 people:

Cost = 30 hours preparation + 50 hours attendance (0.5 hours x 100 people)

That's 80 hours. A 30-minute presentation costs two working weeks! And if it does not result in a change, that's two wasted weeks.

Let's briefly recap what we've said about action:

1. In the chapter on goals, we established that the main goal of your presentation is what people will *do* as a result of hearing it. So, start your preparation by asking yourself: what action should people take as a result of my presentation?
2. In the chapter on ending your presentation, I said that you had to speak out your *"call to action"* (C2A) as clearly as possible; *tell* people what you want them to do.

If you tell people a story with a *point,* not only will they listen and remember, they will be moved to *act* - and that's the key to inspiring change.

Coming up...

What do *you* need to be able to tell stories in your presentation? More than that, what do you need to apply *any* of the techniques I'm describing, whether that's a catchy start, a call to action or the STAR moments we'll see later? The answer is: *confidence.* But how can you get confidence in presenting? And what should you do if you are nervous? In the next chapter, we're going to squash presentation nervousness once and for all.

Summary

1. Stories contain the 3Ps: a Person, a Problem and a Point.
2. Stories should not be too long: aim for about 30-60 seconds.
3. Stories keep attention, are memorable and emotional.

Exercise

Tell a story to someone *today*. This might be in a one-on-one chat, in a presentation or in front of a group. Keep it short (15-30 seconds).

Practice this every day for one week. Write down what stories you told, to whom and how long each story took.

#	Story I told (summary)	I told it to (name)	Duration approximately
1			
2			
3			
4			
5			
6			
7			

What stories can you tell in your presentation? In an earlier chapter, you already wrote down stories for each of these:

- the Problem,
- the Cause,
- the Possible Solutions
- the Chosen (or Recommended) Solution.

Here you can write down other stories. You probably shouldn't tell all the stories you think of. But during the preparation, generate lots of story ideas. You can tell stories to help your audience remember your three specific points. And then remove the less powerful ones: *kill your darlings.*

Story ideas:

1.
2.
3.
4.
5.

Speaking at TEDx!

"Always give a speech that you would like to hear."
Andrii Sedniev - author and entrepreneur

This chapter contains spoilers for my TEDx talk. If you haven't seen it yet, please watch it before reading further.

"How to present to keep your audience's attention"

Mark Robinson; TEDxEindhoven

https://youtu.be/BmEiZadVNWY

I arrived early, at about 7 am. I cycled there alone to gather my thoughts in peace. It was a lovely clear, fresh summer morning: Friday 8 July 2016. When I got there, the team were already very busy. Many of them had been up until 3 am setting up the huge gantry for the lights and doing other preparations.

There were four blocks of three speakers, two in the morning and two in the afternoon. Unfortunately for the team, despite all the hard work and great preparations, there were technical problems during the first block which meant the first speakers' slides did not work as planned.

This was hugely frustrating for the team, the speakers and the audience. I felt sorry for them all and hoped these issues would be resolved by the time it was my turn.

In the run-up, we had been asked when we would most like to speak. I chose the final slot of the morning. I had several reasons:

1. People would have my talk fresh in their minds when they went to lunch, so they would be more likely to talk about it.
2. No after lunch dip for the audience (or myself).
3. I could eat my lunch: if my talk was *after* lunch, I would be too nervous.
4. And I wouldn't care if I dropped my entire lunch all over my clothes!

I was waiting off to the side while the previous speaker gave her talk. Sadly, I was not able to concentrate on it as I was far too nervous about mine. I just stood off to the side in the darkness (only the stage was lit) doing Power Poses[43]!

Then suddenly, it was time. The host introduced me, the thunderous music started and I walked into the bright lights of the stage to loud applause. The famous red dot carpet was waiting. I stood on it and began.

"Imagine..."

Very early on I made a mistake. But if you watch the video, you will only get a hint of it. I pressed the button to show the text, *"I have a dream"* a little too early, which of course spoiled the joke. However, thanks to the magic of post-performance video editing, you don't see the screen until *after* I speak those words!

There is another small mistake. This is another reason why it is important to practice in the room where you give the presentation,

---

[43] What are Power Poses? That's coming up in the next chapter!

and especially to go through your slides. There is one line of text which starts, *"That one day..."* On the big screen, the line was too long. So the final word, *"of"* was moved to the next line, on its own. That wasn't intentional - that was due to the different resolution on that screen compared to *every other screen* I'd practiced on. But it didn't matter, it only made the *"Martin Luther King Jr using PowerPoint"* joke funnier.

With the bright lights, I couldn't see the audience very clearly. So when I asked the audience questions, getting them to raise their hands, I had to guess at how many people raised their hands based on the first couple of rows. And when I asked them to shout out answers I couldn't hear the audience's response! So I just said the expected answers like, *"Blackbird aircraft"*, knowing that it would work fine in the video (the people watching online couldn't hear the audience either!).

People often ask me during my workshop what happens if you forget part of your speech? The answer is: very often it doesn't matter. If you forget it, despite all your practice, then it probably wasn't necessary. It's *"killing your darlings"* in real time!

That's exactly what happened to me. In the part about questions, I show how to change normal sentences into questions. I had practiced six questions. But in front of the live audience, I only managed two. Did anyone notice? Of course not. And nor will they notice if you forget a detail of your talk.

(Rereading this chapter, it's funny how much I focus on my mistakes. But that's what every speaker does. As you will see later, that's partly why my workshops focus on positive feedback, because WE are our own worst critic!)

As I've stated, I'm not a natural speaker. If I could redo the talk, I would change one other thing (apart from forgetting the rhetorical questions). I would improve my intonation.

One of my friends asked me afterwards, *"Did you deliberately have a dull voice?"* Sigh. The answer is No, that's just natural for me. (I am an engineer after all!) However, it has turned out to be an advantage: if people will listen to me with *that voice*, because of the techniques that I use, then they will listen to *anyone!*

At TMC we get coaches to help us with our personal development. My coach, Natalia, has enthusiastically told people about my TEDx talk: *"He's an engineer, he's English and he speaks in a monotone voice. You would expect this to be boring. But Mark's talk is truly inspirational."*

And yes, I was nervous the whole time. Would

I remember the speech? Would I freeze up? The only moment I really *started* to relax was after the applause and our host, Callahan, came onstage to ask the prepared question.

We hadn't practiced this, so even though the question was staged, I hadn't planned how to end the exchange!

Fortunately, the answer came to me at that moment. Since I had just explained how to get applause in the final second, I simply repeated that and left the stage to more wild applause!

During lunch, I spoke to several people and got many compliments for my talk. But to be honest I was in a bit of a daze. It was done and it felt like my brain was saying, *"I've been working at 150% for the last two months, now I'm taking a break!"*

I joined my family for the afternoon talks, sitting in the audience. I was so glad that I was done: the months of tension could finally start to dissipate. I could relax somewhat and enjoy the rest of the talks.

At the end, I went out with my family for a wonderful Mexican meal. I drank too many beers and then, at about 8 pm and after a celebratory cigar, fell fast asleep in our garden.

That was one big item off my bucket list. In the following months, another huge item would be crossed off the list...

Help! I'm nervous! Building self-confidence

"Feel the fear of public speaking and do it anyway."
Arvee Robinson - speaker & trainer

Healthy fear

"According to most studies, people's number one fear is public speaking. Number two is death. Death is number two. Does that sound right? This means to the average person, if you go to a funeral, you're better off in the casket than doing the eulogy."
Jerry Seinfeld - Comedian

"You? Terrified?!" While writing this book, I often heard that exclamation when I told people its original title: *"From*

Terrified to TEDx"[44]. But, yes, I was terrified in that first presentation. Yes, I was also pretty nervous on the TEDx stage. And, yes, I still get nervous before any talk in front of a group. And that's a *good thing*. A little nervousness helps me to focus on doing my best, to give the very best speech I can.

Some time ago I gave a speech for which I was too relaxed. In the run-up, I prepared for it but did not practice it much. It was only in the final two days that I started to get genuinely concerned about the talk. Then I really improved my preparation and seriously started practicing out loud. But I only practiced out loud seven times. I think I would have given my speech an 8 or 9 out of 10. If I had been more nervous, I would have prepared better, practiced 10-20 times, and then delivered a 9 or 9.5 / 10 speech.

The talk still went well, but not quite as well as it should have. I had learnt my lesson: even if my nervousness decreases (which it does with experience), I must still *keep practicing*.

So nerves are normal - and even helpful. Almost everyone feels nervous in front of a group. But the secret of public

---

[44] *"From Terrified to TEDx"* was originally going to be the title of this book. I checked with TED and sadly, it's not possible to use *"TEDx"* in a book title in case people think this book is endorsed by TED. For the record, I completely understand and agree with TED's reasons.

speaking and confidence more generally is: be terrified - and do it anyway!

How then can you build confidence in front of a group? This chapter will give you several ways to boost your confidence and reduce, but not eliminate, your nerves.

Practice

"If you're not comfortable with public speaking - and nobody starts out comfortable; you have to learn how to be comfortable - practice. I cannot overstate the importance of practicing."
Hillary Clinton - American politician: former First Lady and Secretary of State

A bit of a no brainer this: as stated when we discussed preparation, you must *practice* your presentation. Even if the presentation sounds great *in your head*, you must speak it out loud. Practice at least ten times, preferably in the room where you will deliver your presentation.

But also, practice giving presentations whenever you get the chance. Better yet, *make opportunities*. Present at work and at social events. Join your local Toastmasters or a similar group. Practice speaking in groups, making use of the exercises in this book.

Over time and with practice, it *will* get easier. This will not happen overnight so take a long-term view. As you get better and better at presenting, your confidence will certainly increase (both on stage and off).

Not a monster

When we see a huge audience, something in our brains says, "Monster!" Rather than seeing a hundred or so separate people, we just see one huge *thing* in front of us. Maybe because, in the moment, that's all our brains can handle.

How does this affect us as presenters? I've seen presenters range from losing eye contact with the audience to a full-blown panic attack.

How can we avoid this? Realise that you are speaking *with a collection of individuals*. You don't have to feel any more nervous in front of a group than in front of one. You are having an (admittedly, one way) conversation with many of them *at the same time*.

So when you stand on the stage, take a moment to make eye contact with a few of them before you start speaking. And remember: they are not a monster; they are people, just like you and me.

Power pose

My daughter's 12th birthday was celebrated with her friends at a park where they could climb through trees on specially designed courses. The children were all safely clipped to a steel cable so that they could not fall, but nor could they overtake each other. At the end of many of these courses was a zip wire. The first time she encountered this, my daughter was very scared.

However, I knew exactly what to do... or so I thought. I called up to her (several metres above my head) and said, *"Come on, I'll count to three and then you jump! One, two, three, JUMP!"*

Nothing happened. I repeated this multiple times, including various bribes and, eventually, threats.

Still nothing. Meanwhile, a queue of impatient children (mostly her birthday invites) formed behind her.

Then my wife came over. *"Do a power pose!"* she said. *"As if that will help!"* I thought. *"That's just one of those things trainers (like my wife) say!"*

But, after a 90-second power pose, my daughter jumped onto the zip wire and went down, no problem.

Since then I've included Power Poses in my workshop. I've told this story to multiple groups and often there is one person who has a similar story to tell. One time there was a musician who said that he and his band did power poses just before going on stage.

I was once at a theatre to give a presentation on stage. As I was waiting in the wings along with several other *"professional"* presenters, I started to feel more nervous. So I, rather self-consciously, started to do a power pose. Then I looked around at my fellow presenters - they were all doing the same thing! Even pros get nervous before giving a presentation.

So what is a power pose and why does it work?

What is a power pose?

Stand up. Yes, really do this! You will get the most out of this part if you experience it.

Stand up and, in a moment, close your eyes. Imagine you've just run and won a marathon. After hours of running, you cross the line first, exhausted but triumphant. You raise your arms in the air, with fists clenched! Do that - raise your arms above your head, imaging you've just won a marathon.

Now hold that position for two minutes. That's a power pose[45].

At least, that's one of them. There is a variant where you stand with your legs slightly apart and your hands balled into fists, on your hips. That's called the *Wonder Woman*.

For an extra boost, combine it with the first exercise in this book: visualise your presentation as a great success.

Why does a power pose work?

When you're happy, you smile. Similarly, your body works the other way: when you smile *first*, you become happier.

And the same applies to the power pose. When you've done a massive achievement (won a marathon), you adopt the power pose because you *feel powerful*. So if you start with the power pose, you will have a feeling of more power. But *does* this work? Since it was popularised, there has been an ongoing debate. The latest research backs up the fact that a power pose *does* increase feelings of power.

---

[45] See Amy Cuddy's TED talk, *"Your body language may shape who you are"* (TED.com) https://www.ted.com/talks/
amy_cuddy_your_body_language_may_shape_who_you_are

My recommendation is that you try it for yourself. If you think it works, that it gives you a feeling of power, then for you it does work. It works for me.

When should you do a power pose?

Do a power pose in the 15 minutes or so before you present. Go somewhere you won't be seen, like a nearby toilet, and raise your hands high above your head. Imagine you've just walked offstage and your speech or presentation went really well. Hold that pose for two minutes.

Smile

Smile! Smile before you walk on stage as you greet the people who organised the event whether that's your boss or the conference organisers. Smile at your audience as they walk in; you are already creating a warm bond with them. You will realise that your audience is made up of normal people, it is not a monster (see above). This will increase your confidence.

And as we've just seen, your body follows your posture. So smile genuinely before your presentation and feel your happiness, and confidence, increase.

Admit your nerves

This seems counter-intuitive: *"Admit your nerves?! You mean, tell my audience that I feel nervous? Won't I seem weak?"*

No, quite the opposite. Recently I saw a manager do exactly that. In front of a small group (about 20 people) he said, *"Normally I don't feel nervous, but today I do."*

Do you think we thought less of him? On the contrary, it was *brave* of him to admit that. Doing so gave him several huge benefits:

1. We could identify with him because we could also feel nervous in that situation. People like to feel that they can identify with the speaker. And speakers are more persuasive when the audience thinks, *"That person is like me."*
2. And because we could identify with him, we are more likely to be more lenient towards him.
3. He lowered expectations but not in a bad way. Anything he does now is good!
4. Attention level goes up. Why is he nervous? What will he say? Will this go badly wrong then? Yes, waiting for something to go wrong is interesting - and will keep our attention!
5. We feel flattered: *"He is nervous in front of us? Wow, we must be important!"*
6. He becomes more authentic. He started by showing us his true self. Now he has nothing to hide and so he will become more confident.

Glass of water

> *You are in front of your audience about to make your third and final point. And... you've forgotten it. What was that crucial point? Your mind has gone blank. Meanwhile, there are many pairs of eyes all looking up at you, watching, waiting... Someone gives a little cough which breaks the silence. You start to sweat. You start looking through your notes... what was it?! You look up at the audience. One of them looks at their watch...*

That's what we want to avoid. But how? First, you should know that having a mind blank in front of an audience is not weird, it is normal. And so, we can prepare for it.

Here is a simple trick: have a glass of water near you. When you have a mind blank, reach out and take a sip of water. For your audience, this is a natural break of 3 - 5 seconds. Nothing strange, presenters often get a dry throat and take a sip of water. It will also give your audience more time to consider what you've just said. And that short silence also increases people's attention.

For you though, it feels like 30 seconds! 30 seconds of *thinking time* where your brain will race and, almost always, come up with that point you had momentarily forgotten. You put down your glass, speak your next sentence, and no one realises your mind briefly went blank.

And always remember...

Always remember: you are the one presenting probably because you know more than anybody else in the room on the subject. That's why you're the one on stage and they're not! So remember that fact and draw strength from it: you're the expert.

Coming up...

When you think about presentations, what's the first thing you think about? Many people think about one specific, well-known tool. It's a tool which whole presentation skills books are dedicated to, a tool without which many people would not dare to present. And yet, treated badly, it's a tool that can destroy your presentation by making it into a boring and confusing data dump.

It's also a tool which, up until now, I've largely ignored.

In the next chapter, we'll tackle it head-on. We're going to talk about the elephant in the room... PowerPoint.

Summary

1. Nerves are normal and are a *good thing*. They help you to do your best during the preparation.
2. Nerves may never go away entirely but may be brought under control by practice, realising you are speaking with individuals, a power pose, smiling or simply admitting to your audience that you feel nervous.
3. Forgot what you were going to say? Take a sip of water.

Exercise

Think about an upcoming event in which you might feel nervous. It may be a conversation with a difficult colleague, an important meeting or even a presentation. Try out the techniques mentioned in this chapter, for example:

- practice (out loud) what you might say
- realise they are people a lot like you
- do a power pose
- smile at the other participants in the run-up
- confess your nerves

And have a glass of water on standby!

What will you do before and during your presentation to improve your confidence and reduce your nervousness? Write down your specific plan.

During my presentation preparation, I will increase my self-confidence by...

Right before my presentation, I will lower my nerves by...

If I start to feel nervous during my presentation, I will successfully cope with it by...

66

The first workshops

"Every accomplishment starts with a decision to try."
John F Kennedy - POTUS 35

It took nearly a month for my talk to go online. There was a whole editing process for all the talks and they also have to go through an approval procedure before being published on the official TEDx talks channel[46].

Coincidentally I was on another family holiday when I suddenly got the message: my talk was live! As soon as I could, I went back to my hotel room and watched it. And not only me - since it is an official TEDx talk, many more people have viewed it and are still watching it: it gets hundreds of views every day.

What did my employer make of all this? Well,

---

[46] https://www.youtube.com/user/TEDxTalks

TMC is a special company. Entrepreneurship is in its DNA. And therefore TMC strongly encourages entrepreneurial behaviour in its *"employeneurs"[47]*. So when I got back from holiday and proposed offering evening workshops on presentation skills to my colleagues, TMC strongly supported that. Daan, one of the managers, gave me valuable advice at this stage on everything from pricing to getting customers (and he also sent me many customers, as he still does to this day).

He and my account manager Benjamin both joined my first evening. Together with other TMC colleagues, my first workshop on 7 September 2016 had six participants! The feedback I got was great, so I set about organising several more, including one at the Eindhoven University of Technology for some students, via a TEDx contact.

I gave another evening workshop in October and one in November. Then I got a request from Lucie to join my December workshop. She had only joined TMC a few months before to help in its international business

---

[47] The word is a portmanteau of *"employee"* and *"entrepreneur"*.

development and was eager to develop the skills of the employeneurs. After having experienced the workshop for herself, Lucie quickly joined the group of early promoters within TMC.

I gave a total of five evening sessions at TMC, the final one in January 2017. TMC kindly allowed me to use a meeting room free of charge to try out the concept. At the time, participants would pay TMC which in turn would pay me. Daan stepped up again, encouraging me to develop this concept into my own business and charge customers directly.

When someone encourages you to pursue your ambitions, it can change your life. This suggestion from Daan, and the support I got from TMC and my family, would change *everything*.

The elephant in the room: PowerPoint

"PowerPoint: the unholy love child between Microsoft Word and an overhead projector."
Mark Robinson - software consultant, speaker & author

Should you use PowerPoint? Will it help or hinder your presentation? And if you do choose to use it, how can you get the best out of PowerPoint?

The Dangers of PowerPoint

"Your slides should be a billboard, not a document!"
Lee Jackson - author & speaker

Information overload

Not so long ago I attended a presentation by a senior manager. There were about 30 slides. One of the first slides contained 16 points. I'm not joking, I wish I was. But I sat there and counted them. And the following slide? A mere 15 points.

The whole presentation was about 10 minutes. Then each slide was displayed for an average of 20 seconds. So those two slides of 31 points took 40 seconds: about one point of information per *second!*

And the speaker was talking at the same time! Even more information.

This reminds me of a very old game show: BBC's The Generation Game. Contestants would sit in front of a conveyor belt for 45 seconds. Items would appear from out of sight and then go past the contender, a bit like a baggage carousel at an airport. At the end, every item they could remember, they could keep. Of course, it very quickly became overwhelming: items they'd remembered at the start were quickly forgotten as another item appeared every two seconds.

But that's what many speakers do, especially when armed with PowerPoint. Presenters click their way through slides full of bullet points and expect the poor audience to remember as many items as they can! They present way too much information in too little time. If only, like The Generation Game, it lasted just 45 seconds!

It's a bit like a restaurant: people need time to digest. What you want to offer is a Michelin star approach: multiple small amounts of quality food with time in between each course. Most presentations range from fast food to force-feeding. Give people time to digest the information: use pauses (coming up when we talk about POTUS 44), tell stories and *limit the Education*: kill those darlings!

PowerPoint vs eye contact

I work a lot with technical people and they (OK, *"we…"*) tend to be shy. So, if you give them a screen to stand next to, then it's like a puppy with a bright, shiny ball: they cannot take their eyes off it. And they dare not make eye contact with their audience. So they stand looking at the screen, with their back to the audience.

And… they READ THE SLIDES! AAAAAAAAarrrrrrrgggghh! So therefore they give a BAD (remember that?) presentation.

As a presenter, you have a choice: you can look *either* at your slides *or* your audience, not both. So if you choose to use PowerPoint, remember: it's not about the slides - it's about your connection with your audience. And an important part of that is eye contact. You need to look at them, and they need to look at you, not at your slides: your slides should support your story, not take over it.

So how do you make sure you keep eye contact? Some people do this naturally; I'm not one of those people. So when I'm presenting, I have to think, *"Now I need to look over to this side; now I need to look at the front row, ... "*, to make sure I make eye contact with every part of the audience.

But what about that big bright screen distracting both you and your audience? We'll come back to that in just a moment.

False confidence

Recently I made beautiful slides for a workshop. The slides contained instructions for an exercise for the participants. By creating these *truly beautiful* slides, I felt more confident about my workshop.

However, this can be *false*. If you spend your time prettifying the slides instead of practicing, you will be more confident *until* you appear before the group. Don't waste too much time on your slides. Instead: practice, practice, practice.

Prioritise practicing over PowerPoint!

WYSINWYG

Here's what happens: you spend *hours* creating your slides; when you're finished you step back and admire your handiwork. You've created a sublime work of art... without doubt, you know that one day your slides will be featured in The Louvre, alongside the Mona Lisa. That's how good they are.

However, when you stand to give your presentation, the slides don't work as you expect. I've seen all the following occur:

- the text did not appear as expected (because the screen aspect ratio is not the same as what you prepared)
- some slides don't appear at all (this can occasionally happen with certain images or fonts: they appear on the laptop, but not on the screen)
- videos don't play as expected (either choppy video, sound problems or they don't play at all, especially if they rely on an internet connection)

In short: WYSINWYG: What You See Is Not What You Get.

There is one solution to all these (well, apart from not using PowerPoint at all). You must test your slides in the room you will give the presentation with exactly the same setup:

- same screen
- same laptop
- same sound system
- same clicker or presenter (the handheld device to advance the slides)

Test, test and test everything! Failure to do so will almost *guarantee* something will go wrong in your presentation. But if you successfully test everything in advance, not only will everything go well but also you will be more confident when you start to speak: you *know* your slides won't let you down.

To stress the point further: if you don't test and your slides do fail, you will experience a loss of confidence in front of your audience which is an awful experience. And with good preparation, it is entirely preventable.

Why do so many people use PowerPoint?

"People use PowerPoint like a crutch. But we were born to run!"
Mark Robinson - software consultant, speaker & author

Do we even consider an alternative? Since everyone else uses it, shouldn't we just follow the crowd?

I believe PowerPoint is hugely overused and 95% of presentations would benefit from not using it. But people don't stop to ask if they *should* use it. They just do, because everyone else does.

But another, more subtle reason is: presenters do not *"kill their darlings"*. As a result, they have too much to say, and hence too much to remember. Since they cannot remember everything, they put all their content into slides, where they can read their notes to their bored audience. But if *you* can't remember your presentation while you are giving it, what chance does your audience have of remembering it when you're done?!

Kill your darlings! Focus your message.

The Naked Presenter

Can you guess what comment I hear most during my workshop? During the morning the participants deliver their prepared presentations, usually using PowerPoint. Then, about halfway through the day, the participants suddenly say something like, *"We've been doing presentations completely wrong"*. By the end of the day, almost everyone will drop PowerPoint for their final presentation.

The difference is amazing: the participants, of course, make more eye contact because they are not distracted by a large screen behind them. And the *message* is transformed: they speak with a clear, far more focused message.

But more than that: the morning presentations are often very technical and therefore hard to understand. But in the afternoon, the other participants listening to the more focused message will typically say, *"Oh,* now *I get it!"*

But even that is not the biggest change. When the participants have a focused message and more eye contact, they will speak more passionately about their topic. They *feel* their message - and their audience does as well.

Taken all together, this means they will make a much better connection with their audience. I'm often staggered by the change in just one day.

And a big part of that is dropping PowerPoint. Now, in a moment I will give you a few tips if you still decide to go ahead with it. And if you do, that's OK. I will even show you the few occasions when I think using slides can benefit your message.

But my advice and the most important advice of this chapter is this: **learn to speak without PowerPoint**. You've heard of The Naked Chef? Be The Naked Presenter! Most of the time slides only hinder your message rather than helping it. Use your preparation time to clarify your message (kill your darlings) instead of creating slides.

You may be thinking: *'I can't leave PowerPoint, I need it.'* You might even be feeling scared about presenting without slides. My advice: *Just Do It!* Preferably in a safe environment first, like on your own, in front of your family or on a presentation skills workshop. Throw away the crutch. Stop hobbling, start running! Experience the new freedom of giving a presentation without PowerPoint. It will be *so refreshing* for your audience as well!

Go naked! Present without PowerPoint.

No PowerPoint? Then what's the alternative?

The alternative is a flip chart. What benefits does a flip chart have over PowerPoint?

First, it forces you to focus your presentation. You can no longer show 80 slides full of text... now you have to focus on a few key words. It automatically helps you to *kill your darlings*.

Secondly, you have to slow down your presentation. It takes a few moments to write a few words or draw an image (that's coming later) on a flip chart. During that time people's brains have a chance to catch up. It's a completely natural pause, a chance for everyone to take a breath. The conveyor belt of information is empty for a few seconds.

Thirdly, it adds to the mystery. At the start of one of my workshops, a presenter explained how to create a great barbecue (Empowerment!) using PowerPoint. At the end of the workshop, after he'd learnt a number of new techniques, he gave a new version of his presentation using a flip chart. He started by drawing the barbecue on the paper. It wasn't a perfect drawing but it didn't have to be: it was much more interesting than showing a slide. He built up the picture, adding first hot coals and then cold ones around the edge, giving his presentation an *"organic feel"* as he added to the image.

If you've never tried to communicate your message with a flip chart, do it! It will feel liberating. Your message will be more focused and much easier to listen to. And it will stand out amongst all the standard PowerPoint presentations.

Are there *any* circumstances when you *should* use PowerPoint?

If your office / work experience is anything like mine, you would be forgiven for thinking the answer to this question is: *"You should* always *use PowerPoint!"*

But my answer is: *"You should almost never use PowerPoint!"*

However, here are the few occasions when slides can help your presentation:

Presenting data

For example, you can show a relevant graph. But be careful! Watch out for these points:

1. People will not remember the data in detail, so you need to highlight the main point you want to convey. Why are you showing them this information? Does it help your goal? If not, it's a darling... and you know by now what we do with them.
2. Your audience may draw a different conclusion from your data than you do. So ensure you have it reviewed first with the experts.
3. Make sure your graph is readable! Sounds silly, but I've seen unreadable data many times, especially at the back of the room. This is another reason to test your presentation in the room in which you will present!
4. Remove *all* unnecessary text! Do you really need the axes labels, the text showing the data points, the graph title? Or will you explain it verbally? This has advantages: you can lead your audience through the data, explaining what you want to highlight.
5. Give your audience the time to process it. You can do this with a direct command. *"Take 20 seconds to examine this graph."* And then keep quiet! People

can't process this and listen to you. Note: tell them how long it will take to avoid the silence becoming awkward.

Showing a picture

On a few occasions, photographers have joined my workshop. They have shown their own beautiful pictures. But again, watch out! If you do show a picture:

1. Only show pictures if they add to your talk, if they help your goal.
2. Do not show any text with the picture.
3. Give people a few seconds to process the picture. During this time, stand to one side; allow people to focus 100% on the picture.
4. Then give your voice over. Use *your voice* instead of text on the slide.
5. After you've made your point, make the screen go black and let the focus return to you. We'll talk more about that in a moment.

Where can I find decent images?

If you decide to use PowerPoint to show images, where can you find professional ones you can use?

Here are a few great sites for beautiful, free images:

1. https://unsplash.com
2. https://www.pexels.com
3. https://pixabay.com
4. https://www.freeimages.com

5. https://www.flaticon.com (free icons, particularly useful when you want to give all your slides the same "look and feel" but have different icons for each topic)

Each site has its own requirements for using these photos (e.g. photographer attribution) and they change from time-to-time. Please check before use.

You can also make your own drawings. You may think that they won't look that professional. However, they can be powerful: they are fun, show us a little bit about your character and hence help you connect to your audience.

We'll talk more about drawings later: they are a STAR moment.

Showing a video

Videos can be really powerful: they always get attention. (Ask any parent: put on a screen and children are magically drawn to it.) But as with every element of your presentation, always ask if it helps your goal.

However, there are a few potential pitfalls; videos often go wrong in presentations. Here's how you can avoid that:

1. Download the video! Do not rely on an internet connection: it is simply one more thing that can go wrong. So download it and embed it in your presentation.
2. Ensure the video is set to start **Automatically**, not via a mouse or keyboard click. This is so that, if you

are using a pointer to advance the slides, you can activate it without walking back to your laptop.

3. You must test it first, in the room using the screen and sound system as provided. How many times have you seen a flustered presenter struggling to show a video and ultimately giving up? So check and double-check *in the presentation room!* When the video is playing during your test, walk around the room to check it can be seen *and heard* in every part of the room. You will probably think to check the visual but make doubly sure to check the audio. I have lost count of the number of times I've seen *one and a half videos*: at first half of the video is shown while the presenter struggles with the sound and then the presenter restarts the video with the sound. It looks unprofessional... because it *is* unprofessional!

4. Introduce the video by explaining briefly why you are showing the video and how long it is. People will relax, knowing how long you are expecting them to watch.

5. Then, get out of the way! Join the audience by standing near them. Watch the video with them. Then they can focus *entirely* on the video.

6. After the video ends, the screen should go black as you go back on stage. Then the audience focus shifts its attention naturally from the video back to you, which is where you want it.

Giving instructions

If you are leading a workshop, you may want to give everyone a few minutes to complete a task. To ensure everyone knows what to do, put the instructions on the screen *after* you've explained them so that your audience can refer to them during the exercise.

Why not show the instructions as you are explaining them? Because people will read the instructions and not listen to you.

Information Channel

Finally, this reason is not for presenters but I've added it for completeness. Companies often use PowerPoint as an *information channel* in their receptions and conferences use these during breaks in presentations. It's simply a series of slides with a timer. Every 30 seconds the next slide is shown. It is used to display useful information, company slogans and so on.

Tips for using PowerPoint

The two commandments

Commandment 1:	**only use PowerPoint when you must**
Commandment 2:	**delete every unnecessary word and slide**

Commandment 1 was already covered in the previous section: do you *need* to use PowerPoint? Will it benefit or hinder your message?

Let's take a moment with Commandment 2. Why is it important? And how can you determine what is unnecessary?

How to earn a fortune

It is important to delete every word and slide that does not help your message because *every second* your audience is looking at your slides they are not looking at and listening to you! And you are presenting yourself and your message: your slides are only there to support you.

So, what should you delete? Here is a simple mental trick to help you. Imagine I will give you £100 (or $ or €) for every word you delete. (I won't by the way... just imagine!) This simple mental trick will help you look really carefully at every slide and remove everything that does not help your goal.

(By the way, you can also use this trick with every email you write.)

You can also apply it to whole slides: imagine I will give you £10000 for every *slide* you delete. So many times, especially at conferences, I see *junk* slides that add nothing to the message. Get rid of them!

(And earn £10000 for every email you don't send!)

Black screen

As a presenter, you want the focus either on you or on your slides. But never on both at the same time. So, when you are speaking (unless you are directly pointing out something on a slide), the slide should be black (or blank, so it looks like the projector is switched off).

This is worth emphasising: either your audience will be listening to you or they will be reading their slides. But they can't do both at the same time. You are in charge during your presentation, so you get to decide what you want them to do. If you want them to look at your slide, keep quiet (unless you are leading them through the information on it). If you want them to listen to you, make the slide go black.

To do this, simply press B for Black. At least, do that if you have an English language operating system. For other languages, the letter varies. For example, for Dutch it is Z for Zwart, for French it is N for Noir. Alternatively, if you have a handheld pointer (also called a presenter), this will likely have a button you can press to make the screen go black.

Make the screen go black *in this way* when your presentation has an unplanned interruption e.g. a question that you want to answer.

But for planned moments, use a black slide.

Here's what I mean. Compare X (pressing B) & Y (having a built in black slide):

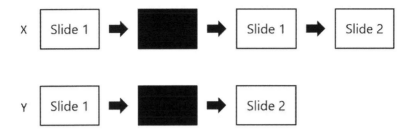

Y looks more professional. So use this unless you specifically want to talk about something else on Slide 1 before going to Slide 2.

Recently, I was asked to speak at an event in front of about 100 guests. Beforehand one of the organisers asked me, *"Mark, I think I already know the answer but I still have to ask... will you be using PowerPoint?"* Of course, I answered, *"No, thanks."*

I was the third of four speakers. All the others used PowerPoint. The organisers had therefore created introduction slides for each of us: the event name and logo together with our name.

So when I went on stage, there was a bright slide with my name on, distracting the audience from me, and hence from my talk.

It so happened that the host was sitting close by, behind the laptop with the slides. So I began like this, *"Before I start my talk, I need our host to do something for me."* Then, to the host, *"Can you please press the B button?"* He looked a little puzzled, then pressed it. The screen went black. Then I said to the audience, *"Press B to make your screen black. And that's the only PowerPoint tip you will ever need!"* So my talk started with laughter and applause!

Laser pointer

The traditional PowerPoint presenter stands in front of his slides... he wants to point out something and reaches for his laser pointer. But he's nervous. He's shaking. He hits the laser button. It's like an 80s techno disco! Lights flashing across the screen as he tries to point the laser at one particular word while shuddering uncontrollably. It's bad.

Or, he could have pressed *Ctrl-L*. This changes the mouse pointer into a laser. Not only does it not shake, but it is also useful if you have more than one screen (common at conferences with a large hall) or if you are presenting online.

And, when you turn to face the audience, the chances of lasering someone's retina with your handheld clicker is zero.

Plus, those laser pointers don't work on LCD screens. But Ctrl-L works!

The only disadvantage is that you have to stay standing behind your laptop (see why this is a disadvantage when we talk about space, later).

Jump to specific slides

You're at the end of your presentation. It has gone as well, no, better than planned! The audience gives you a standing ovation. As the applause dies down, you give your new admirers a chance to drink even more at your fountain of knowledge: *"Are there any questions?"* you ask.

Then someone says, *"Yes, I've got a question about your second slide."*

What should you do? You want to press Up, Up, Up multiple times to go back through all your slides and animations to slide 2. But that's going to look bad. The mystique you've built up is at risk.

Have no fear, the answer is simple. You press 2 followed by Enter and your presentation jumps to slide 2. Question about slide 13? You press 1, 3, then Enter. As long as you know the slide numbers (so have a list of them with numbers to hand), you can jump straight to the correct slide.

Presenter mode

Why do so many presenters have so much text on their slides? Sometimes it's because they want to email their PowerPoint after the presentation. But if we can get all the information from the slides...what is the added value of the person presenting?! Yep, zero.

Or some presenters put text on their slides because they are afraid they will forget what they are going to say. But as

I already wrote, if they can't remember what they will say, what is the chance that the audience will remember all the details of the presentation? Again, zero.

However, if a presenter is scared they will forget because of nerves (instead of just having too much content), help is at hand with PowerPoint's Presenter mode.

Here's how it works: your current slide is shown on the left of your laptop screen. So this is what is shown to your audience on the main screen. The next slide (or animation) is in the top right. And the bottom right contains your speaker notes. **So you don't have to put your speaker notes on the slide!** You just add them underneath your slides when you edit your PowerPoint. And there's even a timer!

But there is a problem: if you are looking at your laptop you are breaking eye contact with your audience. So position your laptop so that its back is towards your audience. Then you can glance easily from your audience to your laptop and back.

I don't like to rely on technology for my notes: I've seen too many technical problems including the laptop crashing. So if I use notes, I like to have them on paper. More on paper notes later.

All the other PowerPoint tips

Want to see all the other tips PowerPoint has to offer? Start your presentation and press F1. (Yes, it's weird that this help dialog only appears when you are running a presentation, because that is the one time you would not want to use it!) A dialog will pop up with various tips, including the ones mentioned above.

Finally...

I was once in a hall with about two hundred other engineers watching a manager give a presentation on a huge screen. Suddenly a message dialog popped up in the bottom right of the display, on top of his slide:

```
                  Get haircut
```

His back was to the screen so he wasn't aware why his audience suddenly started laughing.

Don't let your laptop interrupt your presentation! Close every application except PowerPoint (especially calendar reminders). And put it in Airplane mode. What's the only thing worse for a presenter than *"Get haircut"*?

```
              Your computer will now
              restart to install updates
```

Coming up...

We've talked about presentations... but what about pitches? What should you wear? How can you sound enthusiastic? How should you title your presentation? What phrases should you avoid in your speech? Should you use notes? And what if your boss tells you to give a presentation in an hour, for which you have done no preparation?

The next chapter will answer all these questions - it's packed full of small but powerful tips.

Summary

PowerPoint is often used as a crutch. Don't use it unless you must, because you want the focus to be on you, not on your slides. But if you **must** use PowerPoint:

1. Delete *every* unnecessary word and *every* unnecessary slide.
2. Test your slides! Test using the screen on which you will give the presentation.
3. Especially test video *and audio!*
4. Press B for black when you want the focus back on you (or build in a black screen).
5. Use Ctrl-L for laser pointer.
6. Type a number then press Enter to jump to that slide.
7. Use Presenter Mode to see what's coming next, for your notes and for the timer.

Exercise

Start any PowerPoint presentation and press F1. Look over the tips and choose just one you think is useful. Try it out: pretend you are in front of a group and use that tip. Once you've memorised that tip, repeat for other tips.

Have you already created slides for your next presentation? Go over them again now. What can you remove? Remember: imagine you will get £100 per word and £10000 per slide you delete.

Do you dare to remove them all and become a Naked Presenter?

Here is a list of PowerPoint tips that I've learnt and can implement ...

1.

2.

3.

4.

5.

Should I use PowerPoint?

Here are some ways in which PowerPoint will help my presentation:

And here are some ways in which PowerPoint will get in my way:

Then select one of the following:

☐ *I will dare to give my presentation without PowerPoint*
☐ *This time I will stay with PowerPoint*

Finally, if you are using slides, try deleting words (£100) or whole slides (£10K).

The total amount I earned is:

"

Mark Robinson Training

"And the day came when the risk to remain tight in a bud was more painful than the risk it took to blossom."
Anais Nin - author

A man with a plan

In the first quarter of 2017, I started to set up my own business: Mark Robinson Training. So I decided I'd do something that doesn't come naturally to me: I created something called *a plan*.

Well, actually it was a checklist of items, each marked with the month by which I wanted to complete them: January, February or March of 2017. These were things like: arrange a website[48], register at the Chamber of Commerce, design a style for the site and my invoices, set up the workshop day, set up a bank account, register for VAT, work out email from my new website and publicise!

This plan turned out to be surprisingly powerful. Rather than procrastinating, I got on with it and followed my plan so that I could launch a workshop in April.

Each of these points was new to me. I knew nothing about websites and WordPress, the software used to create websites. I had no idea about the Chamber of Commerce, VAT or even how to set up a business bank account. But as with learning every new skill, you do the research, ask for advice and then *just start*[49].

The challenging part was publicity. How could I get people interested in the workshop?

---

[48] https://www.markrobinsontraining.com
[49] To read more on my *"Just Start!"* mindset, check out my article: https://www.linkedin.com/pulse/just-start-mark-robinson

First-ever full-day workshop

To run a workshop, you need: a time, a place, content and customers.

For the **time**, I booked a day of holiday. That was easy!

TMC helped with the **place**. I spoke with my account manager, Benjamin, and he was happy to provide a room at TMC for me to use without charge. As I said, TMC only *encourages* entrepreneurial behaviour in its *employeneurs*. (Since this behaviour only makes better employees, because they become more proactive and great ambassadors for your company, why don't all businesses do this?!)

I developed the **content** based on my experience from Remco's course, my own ideas from my 15 years of practical experience, the TEDx experience and the evening workshops, together many other sources, including persuaders like Scott

Adams (of Dilbert[50] fame) and the public speaking legend, Dale Carnegie.

But how was I going to get **customers**?

I put the date on my new website and advertised it via LinkedIn. I heard nothing for weeks. Would I quietly drop the idea? Then I got a phone call. It was from Sandra, a student at the Eindhoven University of Technology. One of her fellow students had seen my TEDx talk and recommended it to her. She asked if I gave presentation skills workshops?

By this time it was only a couple of weeks before the course. I told her that I had one planned but I wasn't sure it would go ahead because of a lack of participants. But she offered a solution: that she would try to get more people.

And she did! On Friday 21 April 2017 at TMC, eight students including Sandra walked into my very first presentation skills workshop: **Present with Confidence!** rebranded the following year as **Powerful Presentations!**

---

[50] https://dilbert.com

Beforehand I had asked them all to prepare a five-minute presentation on any topic. So on the morning of the workshop, I alternated between theory (what you find in this book) and one of the participants delivering their prepared presentation. So for example, it was:

- what makes a great presentation (3Es)?
- *participant presentation*
- what should be the goal of your presentation?
- *participant presentation*
- how to prepare a presentation?
- *participant presentation*

and so on. That variation is what helped keep people focused the whole day. It's why I decided on a similar approach for this book, alternating between theory and story.

I remember them commenting more than once that I was a *"Presentations Jedi"* because often, when they asked a question, the next theory part exactly answered their question!

In the afternoon, they presented the theory back to each other. Finally, they put it all into practice for their closing presentation. They all followed the pattern I've now seen hundreds of times: the final presentation was dramatically better than the first! They had:

- a catchy start,
- a clear goal,
- a great structure,
- a personal story
- a call to action and
- no PowerPoint!

Some of them even added a STAR moment. And all of them *killed their darlings!* Lots of unnecessary *fluff* was removed to make much more focused and clear messages.

And do you know what comment I hear the most often during my workshop, between people's first and last presentations on the day? It's this:

"I'm going to redo my presentation completely!"

Back to that first workshop: I'm pleased to report that, when they learned that this was my *first* full-day workshop, they were amazed! And the *average score* from all participants was 9/10!

Mark Robinson Training had started, I was an entrepreneur. So how could I get more customers? How could I increase the momentum? And was the 9/10 score the limit or could it go even higher?

99

A treasure chest of extras

"If you can't communicate and talk to other people and get across your ideas, you're giving up your potential."
Warren Buffet - investor and philanthropist

"A treasure chest of extras" sounds better than *"Miscellaneous"*. And it's all about the *presentation*, right?

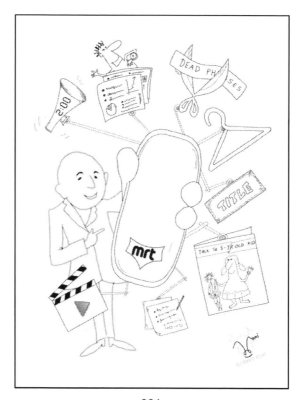

Presentation notes

Should you use notes in your presentations? Or should you rely on your memory? The answer is... it depends. You will only need to use your notes if you cannot remember your presentation. So, how confident are you in your presentation and your ability to deliver it?

- **Confidence level: low.** Take your entire speech written out with certain keywords highlighted. This will enable you to look at the highlighted keywords if you forget what you were going to say and also fall back on reading your script if all else fails. Hopefully, you won't need that but just having the full script on standby will give you more confidence.
- **Confidence level: medium.** Here you just need a list of keywords, with maybe a couple of extra explanatory words per keyword. (Alternatively, take a mind map.) This will enable you to make more eye contact with your audience and speak more naturally. If necessary, you can glance at your notes to know the next part of your speech.
- **Confidence level: high.** You have no notes. You know your topic well, have lots of speaking experience and are not afraid to *"think on your feet"*. When you've given a few speeches without notes, you are a Presentation Jedi! But if you are at this level, don't get overconfident. You must still prepare well and *practice!*

Make sure to number the pages of your written notes. Why is that? Many years ago I read a small book on presenting that explained this perfectly. It said, *"Number your note pages. This is so that,* when *you drop them, you can quickly put them back in order."*

What should I wear?

"Take clothing advice from a software consultant at your own risk!"
Mark Robinson - software consultant, speaker & author

Choose clothes that make you feel *confident.* This is important because your level of confidence will directly impact the persuasiveness of your message. Your self-confidence inspires others' confidence both in you and in your message.

But always choose clothes within the parameters of your culture, both company culture and country culture. So if you are expected to wear a suit, do so. If adding your favourite bright red tie makes you feel confident, add that. Dress to impress, but especially to impress *yourself.* Give yourself that extra confidence boost!

Give this presentation in an hour; here are the slides!

Have you ever been given a PowerPoint slide deck and told to present it? You search through someone else's incomprehensible slides, filled with dull text and bizarre diagrams, rearranging what you can, desperately trying to eke out a message... It's like trying to pan for gold in a cat litter tray: you feel dirty, there is no gold and the owner just gets annoyed with you.

Recently I experienced exactly this. I had to present a technical topic with *one hour's notice!* So I glanced through the 60 or so slides and decided *no, I am not going to do this.* This was a topic I knew well[51]. So I gave it some thought and then hatched a plan. I went across town to the office where the group of 15 participants were waiting.

In the presentation room, I started by asking a few check questions: what did they already know? Of the three topics I was asked to speak about, they already knew the first two.

This was a great time saver. So, to set expectations, I told them, *"We have two hours reserved for this slot but based on what you already know we should be done in less than half that time."*

I then went to the flip chart and gave them a 10-minute introduction to the remaining topic. Then I asked for questions. The rest of the time was pure interaction: they asked me questions and I answered them. Sometimes I asked them questions.

---

[51] This is important for what comes next. If you don't know the topic well, my advice is to say *"No"* and just email the slides. In that circumstance, what possible value can you add as a presenter?

The result? This was a presentation perfectly tailored to their needs. And it kept their attention because it was interactive.

The feedback we received after the workshop was interesting. People loved the format (flip chart instead of PowerPoint). But to my surprise, many people commented on how well prepared I was!

The lesson here is: when you are given someone else's slides to present, you don't have much time but you know the topic well:

1. Ditch the slides.
2. Explain the basics.
3. Do a Q&A (questions and answers session).

Remove dead phrases

There are some phrases you should avoid in your presentations. Let's start with examples:

- *"I want to tell you a little bit about..."*
- *"I hope I've given you enough information"*
- *"Sorry, I haven't had much time to prepare."*

What do all these phrases have in common? They all *minimise* your impact by *minimising* your message. They all give the same message to your audience: *"It's just my presentation. It's not going to change your life. It's little. I'm little. You can ignore me."*

You're thinking, *"That's pretty strong!"* right? Or is it? Let's look at the message behind them.

"I want to tell you a little bit about"

This terrible start of a presentation is wrong on so many levels. Why should I care what *you* want to *tell* me? *"Telling me"* sounds like a data dump!

"A little bit" implies it's not very important and can therefore easily be ignored: on a subconscious level you are giving your audience permission to switch off. And if it is *"a little bit"*, why does it take you an hour and 50 slides?!

Replace this with the catchy start mentioned earlier.

"I hope I've given you enough information"

Never say, *"I hope"* in your presentation. It's weak. If you've done your job you *have* given them enough information.

Speaking of which, don't say, *"enough* information*"*. People aren't looking for information; that's never the WII4ME. People are looking to be empowered. Sure, that will necessitate some information, but that is never the goal of your presentation.

So what should you say instead? Replace this weak end with the strong end from the chapter on ending your presentation, including a clear call to action.

"Sorry, I haven't had much time to prepare."

It's never a good idea to apologise for your presentation. And saying you haven't had time to prepare sounds like an excuse and, again, it tells people to switch off. It also implies that you didn't value your presentation or your audience.

If you haven't had time to prepare, use the interactive method mentioned above.

Presentation title?

Often you will need to give your presentation a title. This is always the case at conferences. However, you can also use this for work presentations: if you advertise a title which grabs people's attention and gets them interested, they are more likely to attend.

What kind of title does that?

1. Titles with a question. For example:
    1. How does the Widget 4000 work?
    2. What is our product roadmap for next year?
    3. Why are sales falling and how will we turn that around?
    4. Who is our new head of department? (This is a way for them to introduce themselves.)

2. Titles with a benefit. These often begin with *"how to"*:
    1. How to use our new HR system

2. How to Win Friends and Influence People[52]

3. These are *even better* when they include *why* you want to do that, using words like *"enables"* or *"to"*.
    1. How our new HR system enables you to follow career developing workshops
    2. How to present to keep your audience's attention[53]

Now take a fresh look at this book's subtitle.

Intonation and slowing down: talk to 5-year-olds

I have two weaknesses in my voice:

1. It's monotone by default. I don't have many ups and downs of emotions in my intonation.
2. I think fast and so I speak fast. My mouth is trying to catch up with my brain. This is especially so when *"on stage"* and I'm nervous.

One *"quick fix"* for both is to imagine your audience is made up of 5-year-olds. Think about it: if you were in front of a primary school group speaking, how would your voice

---

[52] The name of a very famous book.
[53] It's a popular TEDx video I recommend... :)

change? You would have to speak slower, right? And you'd have to sound interesting.

Voilà, imagine you are talking to 5-year-olds and your intonation will get much better!

You may be thinking, *'But won't the audience hear that? Won't I sound patronising?'* It's a good idea to try this out with someone before you go live with your presentation. But generally, the answer is *"No"*. To your audience, you will just sound more clear and interesting.

We'll come back to slowing down our speech in the next chapter, when we look at the world expert on pausing.

Two-minute pitch

"OK, you've got two minutes to tell me about your product or service. Go!"

How would you respond if a busy executive told you that? Or what would you say if you had to pitch to a group of potential investors?

As an example, here is the pitch for my business which I have given to many groups.

> What makes a great presentation? Why are so many business presentations so boring? And how can you

ensure that people will give you their full attention from the start to the end of your presentation?

Good morning, my name is Mark Robinson and in the next two minutes, I will show you how you can make your presentations more clear, more focused and much more persuasive.

I'm not a natural presenter. I can remember my first presentation when I was just 13 years old at school: I stood in front of 30 classmates and I was terrified. I was shaking and went completely white. Who here would admit to being nervous before an important presentation?

[Pause for a show of hands.]

Right, it's natural, isn't it? And one of the reasons for those nerves could be that you've never learnt the most powerful techniques for presenting. After giving a popular TEDx talk four years ago, I set up Mark Robinson Training to share these techniques. I've now helped hundreds of people, especially technical people, present clearly, with focus and in a persuasive way that results in action.

Why would you want to develop your presentation skills? There are two reasons:

- for your career - if you can present well you will be seen as the expert on any topic you

speak on and
- for your confidence - if you can speak confidently to a group, then you can speak confidently in any situation, whether at a social event like a party or in a job interview.

So what are you waiting for? There are just four places left in my next workshop. Go to markrobinsontraining.com to sign up today!

Reverse engineering

Let's reverse engineer that pitch and look at the different parts. What if I tell you that a pitch is just a mini-presentation? Then what presentation elements did you spot in my pitch?

These are the elements in chronological order:

1. Catchy start: 3Q + Name + WII4ME
2. Story (can be at any point in the pitch)
3. Problem
4. Cause
5. Possible solutions => build credibility
6. Chosen solution (explain how this fulfils the benefits)
7. C2A

Did you spot them all in my pitch? I had the *catchy start* and the short *story* of my first presentation. I explained a *problem* (being nervous of presenting) and the *cause* (we don't know the techniques of presenting). I changed the *possible solutions* step; I will explain why in a moment. Then I gave the *chosen solution*, developing your skills and I explained two *benefits*. Finally, I give a very clear *call to action* together with a sense of urgency: *"sign up **today**!"*

So what happened to the *possible solutions* step? Well, what is the purpose of that step? It's to explain your thought process. And why is that important? It's to build credibility for your chosen or recommended solution.

But here, since my solution relies on *my* credibility as a trainer, I give you two reasons why I'm credible: a popular TEDx talk and hundreds of people successfully trained.

You must practice your pitch to ensure it fits within the allotted time. But what if you can't fit all these elements into that time?

Let me ask you a related question: of the seven items listed above, which one is non-negotiable? That is, which one *must* be in your pitch?

Before reading the answer below, take another look at those seven items. Which one do you think it is?

The answer is the Call To Action. A pitch always has a reason: you want someone to invest, to buy, to support, to join... it's always a verb, they've got to DO something with your pitch. So you can't kill the C2A darling.

What about the others? Well, you can drop or shorten anything which does not directly help your C2A goal. For example, you don't need to start with three questions: maybe one is enough. And you might not need to introduce yourself: at a pitching event, someone else will call you on stage by name. And so on... kill any darling necessary to fit within the given time.

Just make sure to tell (not ask) your audience exactly what you want them to do, your call to action.

Presenting via video / online

I often get asked, *"Do you have any tips for online presentations?"* This is closely followed by the admission, *"Video conference presentations are so boring!"*

This is true: it is much harder for people to stay focused in a video conference than when they are physically present. This is especially true when you *"share your screen"* and start hitting them with your slide deck. Just picture for a moment: you're in a video conference and the speaker goes from showing you their face to showing you a slide. Can you feel the drop in attention level? We humans need eye contact to stay interested.

There is an obvious solution. Don't show slides, use a flip chart instead. Using a flip chart during a video conference increases attention as much as it does in person.

But that's only part of the solution. Here are my golden video conferencing tips:

1. Ensure each participant is visible on screen. I ask everyone to switch on their camera and I use software[54] which enables everyone to be in view at once.
2. I always stand when I present, even online. This gives me more energy and authority.
3. I also get everyone to introduce themselves. But just a quick intro – no long speeches! And I preferably ask them for something fun, like: give us your name and one reason we can contact you. (Here I give the lead, *"I'm Mark Robinson and you can contact me if you want to know anything about Disney Princesses. I have two daughters – I'm quite an expert!"*)
4. Focus on giving your presentation and get someone else to do the technical side, like admitting latecomers, enabling breakout rooms, changing who has screen control, etc.
5. Your technical preparation and testing should be even more thorough than normal:
   a. Make sure your camera is at eye level so that you are not looking down on your audience.
   b. Clear away any distractions in your background – all the focus should be on you.

---

[54] My personal preference is Zoom (https://www.zoom.us) which not only shows everyone at once, it has the added value of enabling "breakout rooms".

    c.   Test everything, particularly if you are using new software. Get feedback from a test audience.

6. Of the 3 Es, which one needs to be ramped up? *Entertainment!* You've got to pull out all the stops to keep their attention:
    a.   Use even clearer intonation: you just learnt to talk to five year olds, in video presentations talk to *four* year olds!
    b.   Use more questions and ask specific people questions: *"Dave, what do you think of this?"*
    c.   Use more stories, but keep them short.

7. Get plenty of rest. Video presenting is much more tiring than being in person; it's a very different atmosphere. For example, if you tell a joke, you won't hear any laughter if everyone is on mute. When you ask a question, it's a higher threshold for people to respond. All interaction is dampened. This is unnatural and hence it's draining. So go easy on yourself. Don't beat yourself up when the presentation doesn't seem to go so well - you're basing that on the unnatural lack of interaction. And take a good rest after a video presentation.

Coming up...

We're going to look at a surprising pair of modern-day speakers and what we can learn from them. You know both their names. And you probably like one and loathe the other (the world is split about 50/50 as to which one to like and which one to loathe). Both are gifted public speakers but for *very* different reasons.

And they both have one thing in common: they've both held the title President of the United States.

Summary

1. Use notes to increase your confidence. And use fewer notes when you can.
2. Wear what makes you feel confident (within cultural boundaries).
3. If asked to present on short notice, try a Q&A format.
4. Replace weak phrases like, *"I hope I've given you enough information"* with strong phrases, like a direct call to action.
5. Use a catchy title, e.g. a question or *"How to..."*
6. Want to add more clarity and emotion to your intonation? Pretend your audience are five-year-olds.
7. For pitches, use the presentation format and *always* stick to the allotted time.
8. In a video conference, ramp up the Entertainment.

Exercise

Take a moment to think about these eight treasures. Which one was the biggest eye-opener for you? Write it down and then plan what you want to do with it.

For example, you might write down something you wear that makes you confident. Or you might decide to give your presentation to a friend and ask them to look out for a weak phrase. Or you might give your presentation a new, intriguing title.

> *The biggest eye-opener for me in this chapter was:*
>
> *What I've also learnt from this chapter is...*
>
> *This is what I intend to implement from what I've learnt:*

The Flywheel

"Keep moving forward!"
Walt Disney – entrepreneur, animator and
film producer

After the success of the first workshop, I put the second on the calendar and started advertising. At first, nothing. I started to think that this was a failed experiment, that I should cancel the workshop. Mark Robinson Training nearly stopped there.

Then one of my colleagues, Anne, said how much she would appreciate joining such a workshop. Since we got on well together, this gave me the extra incentive to make sure it happened: I just had to make sure we had more participants.

I recruited more TMC colleagues, a few friends and even my wife... in the end, it was another full workshop.

Since those early days, a lot has changed. First, the workshop itself has evolved. Some of the content has been improved but also the way I deliver that content is different.

With the experience I've built up, I'm able to tell more stories and I've added more fun videos to show the group. As a result of this, the *average* participant score[55] has gone up from an excellent 9 / 10 to the stratospheric 9.5 / 10![56]

At the start of 2018, I decided that it was time to hold the workshops at a location outside of TMC. Even though TMC completely supported my business, I wanted Mark Robinson Training to develop its identity outside TMC. In addition, the atmosphere is completely different offsite: people can *focus*. In an office environment, people tend to read emails during the breaks. At an offsite location, breaks are real breaks, where the brain can process the information and just rest.

So I found a local restaurant that serves great food and has a perfect sized meeting room. Since then I've hosted multiple training

---

[55] How? See this article: *"How do you know if you are doing a good job?"* https://www.linkedin.com/pulse/how-do-you-know-doing-good-job-mark-robinson

[56] By the way, what do you think the "9s" most often say I should do to earn a 10? The answer: give them a handout. Well, now they'll get this book. So I'm expecting 10 / 10, minimum!

sessions there. And we always close the workshop with a drink together.

I love the *"flywheel"* idea of Jim Collins[57]: with any business or initiative, the first few iterations are the hardest, like turning a heavy flywheel. But once it is moving, it moves under its own momentum and increasing the speed becomes easier. So the Mark Robinson Training flywheel was moving. I was starting to give more workshops and even in-company training.

But that flywheel was about to get a big burst of momentum.

99

---

[57] See *"Good to Great"* by Jim Collins

Learning from the best: advanced techniques in oratory and persuasion

"The world has the habit of making room for the man whose actions show that he knows where he is going."
Napoleon Hill - author

POTUS 44: the sound of silence

"You have the power to motivate and inspire. Let your enthusiasm shine."
J. D. Crighton - author

When you think about a speech by President Barack Obama, what comes to mind? Here I'm not thinking of the content but rather his delivery: what makes him a powerful speaker? Before we go any further, I want to stress that I'm not making any political points here. To prove that, in the next section of this book we will see what we can learn from his successor. I'm just interested in what makes him a great speaker.

As I've already stated, one of my challenges is that I speak too fast, particularly when I'm nervous. How can we slow down our speeches? In this section, we will learn how the 44th President of the United States (or POTUS) does that. In a later chapter, we will learn from his amazing, I would say unparalleled, use of body language.

Let's look first at speed. We've already covered the importance of making eye contact with individuals, we've talked about smiling and *"talking to 5-year-olds"*. These will all help you in your pacing so that you do not speak too fast.

But what really *inspires* me to slow down is to watch a speech by Obama. He does not speak quickly, nor too slowly: he speaks at a measured pace and *includes natural pauses*. Where most people (including myself) would add an *"um"* or an *"er"*, he often becomes silent for a moment. Why is this so powerful?

First, it gives him crucial thinking time. But second, it gives his *audience* thinking time! Obama takes frequent pauses of just 1-2 seconds. This is just long enough to give your brain a moment to process what he's just said. This is partly why the *"16 points per slide, 84 slides per hour"* data dump approach is so boring. You can't take in information that fast any more than you can get a refreshing drink from a fire hydrant.

Third, that pause makes him look *smart*. Just to be clear, Obama *is* very smart: you don't become POTUS without being one of the smartest people on the planet. But in that moment of the pause, he also *looks* smart to his audience. It's like he is searching for exactly the right word to say at that moment. So when that word comes, we are all the more ready to receive it, because we think: if *he's* taking extra time carefully to choose his next words, then what's coming next will be great. And that's the fourth reason: the pause emphasises whatever follows after it.

I said just a moment ago that he "includes *natural* pauses". However, I don't know if they are *natural*. Does he really need that time to think? Or is he a highly trained speaker, deliberately adding these pauses for dramatic effect? I don't know. But *the pauses work.*

For example, watch the first 2m15s of this on YouTube: *Intern Q&A with the President (a West Wing Week Special Edition)*[58]. He does add a few ums and ahs. But mostly, he just pauses.

And which pause is the most dramatic? I strongly advise you to watch it before reading any further, to avoid a minor spoiler for his speech!

There are many powerful pauses in Obama's speech to the White House interns. But for me, the most dramatic is just after he says, *"When I'm on my deathbed"*. After this, there is a pause of *three seconds!* This is not a sentence you can rush.

But that's not all we can learn from POTUS 44. What about his body language? We'll come to that in an upcoming chapter when we talk about space.

---

[58] https://youtu.be/5IDQDoxXHm0 *"Intern Q&A with the President (a West Wing Week Special Edition)"* (The Obama White House); first 2m13s

POTUS 45: win, win, win!

"If you have an important point to make, don't try to be subtle or clever. Use a pile driver. Hit the point once. Then come back and hit it again. Then hit it a third time - a tremendous whack."
Sir Winston Churchill - British Prime Minister

President Donald Trump is a polarising character: some people love him, some people hate him. Just as in the previous section with Obama, I ask you to put aside your personal feelings for a moment and consider what we can learn from him to improve our presentation skills.

I'm again indebted to Scott Adams for bringing President Trump's *persuasion* abilities to my attention. There is a lot that I could write on this topic but I don't need to; Adams has already done that[59]. Instead, I just want to highlight two things President Trump does that we can use in our presentations:

- the power of repetition and
- the power of positive words

Let's look at each one.

---

[59] See his book: *"Win Bigly"* (Scott Adams).

The power of repetition

Repetition, repetition, repetition... Watch this YouTube video of a Trump rally before he became President: *"Donald Trump Says "Win" 20 Times in 90 Seconds"*[60]. It has to be seen to be believed. At one point he says, *"We're gonna win, win, win!"* You associate his "brand" with winning because he talks so much about it! (And because his surname is "Trump" - when you trump someone, you beat them - you win!)

At every rally, he repeated the same message. You cannot fail to understand his message. Ask yourself this, *"Can your audience say the same of your presentation?"*

Just to prove that video is not an exception, read this *direct quote* from an interview with Donald Trump, also before he was President[61]:

> *"We don't **win** any more. We don't **win** any more in our country, Sean. We don't **win** any more. We used to **win**. We don't **win** any more. We don't **win** with trade. We don't **win** with war, we can't even beat ISIS. And, we're gonna **win**. If I - **win**. I will tell you: if I **win**, we all **win** because we are gonna **win**."*

---

[60] https://youtu.be/RHEEka-0mFA *"Donald Trump Says "Win" 20 Times in 90 Seconds"* (G4ViralVideos)
[61] https://youtu.be/9LR6EA91zLo?t=160 *"Donald Trump's Debates: 5 Mental Tricks You Didn't Notice"* (Charisma on Command)

12 wins, 17 seconds. Say what you like: he's on message. His message is repeated, so it becomes easier to remember. But it also becomes more believable. This is a known phenomenon called *"Cognitive Ease"*. When you hear something often, it becomes easier to process in your brain. And hence you become more likely to believe it.

And Trump's last *"because"* in that quote was probably the Photocopier Effect[62].

The power of positive words

Our words have power. With our words, we can tear people down. We can inflict lifelong injury on people with our tongue. If we tell people over and over that they are stupid, lazy or not good enough, guess what? They start to believe that. Worse: our criticisms can become a self-fulfilling prophecy. People start to become that which we speak into them. People on the receiving end of those words are not set up for a successful public speaking career.

---

[62] The Photocopier Effect is that, when you want someone to do something, you should use the word *because* and then give a reason. This will greatly increase the chance that people will do it. The name comes from an experiment by Harvard social scientist Ellen Langer. She joined a queue for a photocopier and asked the person in front if she could go in front of them, comparing not giving a reason (60% success rate) to giving a reason (greater than 90% success rate, even if the reason was useless, like: *"because I have to make some copies"*). People like to have a reason, it doesn't matter too much what the reason is!

This is partly why my workshop is focused on *positive* feedback (I'll talk more about this *"superpower"* later). We should think very carefully before criticising other people.

As I've studied the topic of persuasion, I've become more and more convinced that what various authors say is true: we make decisions based on our emotions and *then rationalise them with our brains*. In other words: we don't reason things through and then decide. We decide based on our gut feeling, and then our brains justify our decisions. So if you give a positive message like:

- *"We are going to start winning again"*
- *"Let's make America great again"*[63]

people will associate you with winning and greatness. And who doesn't want that?

Take a moment to think: what message are you broadcasting, perhaps subconsciously, through your choice of words? In your conversations, are you giving off a positive vibe? Or are you being negative, for example by complaining, bickering or gossiping? I'm asking this because that will inevitably spill over into your presentations. And it will be a huge advantage to the

---

[63] Which US president had this as their campaign slogan? Not POTUS 45 but POTUS 40: *"The Great Communicator"*, President Ronald Reagan. The difference is the first word.

impact of your speeches on your audience if you come across as positive; someone with an optimistic outlook.

It goes even further. Donald Trump also says things like, *"There's a lot of love here in this room!"* He said that when meeting Puerto Rico hurricane victims[64]. He even said it, when standing next to the then UK Prime Minister, Theresa May, about a NATO summit![65]

Leave your rational thoughts for the moment[66]. Instead, think about the response of those hurricane victims in that room in Puerto Rico. They'd just been complimented; it was positive feedback! I imagine they feel brought together; that they were all part of the same tribe.

Our words have power, *especially* when we speak to an audience. The principles in this book (especially in the next chapter) will magnify that power, giving you a superpower. So use your new power wisely and for good! Build people up, *inspire* them, and watch your influence grow.

---

[64] https://youtu.be/3ce2p4zZ-Fg?t=110 *"Trump praises Puerto Rico hurricane response, hands out aid"* (AP Archive)
[65] https://youtu.be/rzrZIW4iCX8?t=1165 *"Trump and May give remarks after meeting"* (CNN)
[66] As an engineer, I think things like, *"How are you defining 'love' in this context?"* and *"How can you measure the amount of love in a room?"* and *"Is 'a lot of love' more than the average amount?"* This is probably why so few engineers become politicians.

How Donald Trump influenced my TEDx talk

Near the end of my TEDx pitch[67], I used the words, *"lose, lose, lose"*:

> *"Now why am I doing this? It's because I also have a dream. It's a dream based on a conviction that all of us are unique and all of us have a unique message to share. But sometimes we don't dare to, either through nerves or because we just don't know how to present well. So we keep the message to ourselves. And that's a tragedy. We all **lose**. You **lose** and the world **loses** because they don't hear your ideas, your dreams."*

After this pitch, I realised I had made a mistake. The message I was leaving them with was associating myself with losing! I was concerned that, because of that, my pitch would fail. Do you think that's crazy, that we are not so easily influenced? Hold that thought for just a moment while I tell you what happened: I changed my wording for the TEDx talk. Near the end I deliberately said, *"win, win, win"*:

> *"So, why am I telling you this? It's because I also have a dream: a dream based on a conviction that*

---

[67] https://youtu.be/0J9V7uc1CJw *"TEDxEindhoven pitch Mark Robinson May 2016"* (Mark Robinson Training)

*all of you are unique and all of you have a unique message within you. But sometimes you don't know how to share that message so it stays locked inside. And that's a tragedy. Because if you can share that message, everybody **wins**! You **win** because you get a spotlight put on yourself and [on] your ideas. And you gain the kind of self-confidence you can only get through effective public speaking. And the world can **win**, we can **win**, because we get to hear and potentially implement your ideas."*

People who've seen both videos have told me something startling: not only are my *words* different in both videos, but my posture and intonation are different as well. I'm radiating much more positivity at the end of my TEDx talk.

Now let me answer the point; is this real or imaginary? Can you really influence people so easily with your choice of words? During a recent workshop, I explained this idea to the group. Unknown to all of us, one of the participants decided to put this to the test.

Pierre's presentation was about new equipment used in the company's conference rooms. After he finished, we gave our feedback. Many of us (including me) stated that the presentation was easy to follow and the proposed new equipment sounded easy to use.

Then he blew our minds: he revealed that he had deliberately put the word, *"easy"* into his five-minute presentation *20 times!* He had manipulated our thoughts simply by repeating the word, *"easy"*. That's how easy it is![68]

And when you combine repetition with an acronym or an alliteration (coming later), you give persuasive and therefore powerful speeches.

POTUS 42-45

All four POTUSes 42-45 are great communicators in their own way. To prove the power of this book, look at the elections these men won. In each case (if you are old enough to remember), ask yourself who was the best public speaker? Who made the message the clearest? Who connected better emotionally?

> 1992: George Bush or Bill Clinton?
> 1996: Bill Clinton or Bob Dole?
> 2000: George W Bush or Al Gore?
> 2004: George W Bush or John Kerry?
> 2008: Barack Obama or John McCain?
> 2012: Barack Obama or Mitt Romney?
> 2016: Donald Trump or Hillary Clinton?

---

[68] I promise this is true: only after writing this sentence did I realise that I had just influenced *myself* by writing *"easy"* again!

I submit the following: in each of these elections, the person who won was *always* the person who outclassed the other in public speaking. They moved their public, emotionally, and made their message stick.

Do you agree? Here is a simple test of my theory. Answer these four questions about the 2016 US election (the answers are in the footnotes):

1. What was Donald Trump's slogan?[69]
2. What was Hillary Clinton's slogan?[70]
3. Can you name one of Donald Trump's policies?[71]
4. Can you name one of Hillary Clinton's policies?[72]

---

[69] "Make America Great Again!"

[70] Clinton went through several slogans, including *"Stronger Together"*, *"I'm with her"*, *"Ready for Hillary"*, *"Fighting for us"* and, most bizarrely, *"Love trumps hate"*. This last one was baffling for persuasion experts, because it contained her opponent's name (increasing his recognition) and started with the command, "Love trump": **Love Trump!** Anyone who knows about influence will tell you, this is a terrible subliminal message.

[71] At this point, most people say, *"Build a wall!"* Simple and memorable. I remember watching a TV programme showing how even primary school children in the US knew this policy. That's when you know your message is cutting through! But it is extra clever because of *strategic ambiguity*: by leaving out the details, your brain fills them in with whatever appeals to you most. For you the wall might be green, for me red: whatever we'd most like. See this blog post from Scott Adams for more on this: https://www.scottadamssays.com/2017/09/14/i-explain-the-persuasion-president-trump-is-using-on-the-wall-and-daca   or   read   his aforementioned book, *Win Bigly*.

[72] Nope, me neither.

Since my workshop started around the time of this election, I started to ask participants these questions. Everyone knew the answers to 1 & 3. No one could answer 2 & 4[73].

My point is not political; it's purely about the power of public speaking. If you do it right, you can influence, persuade and perhaps even hypnotise your audience. That's the topic of our next chapter.

Coming up...

In the goal chapter, you established what you wanted people to *do* as a result of your presentation. Each of the speakers mentioned in this chapter has led their audiences to action. How do they do that? What techniques can you copy from them to persuade your audience? In the next chapter, you are going to discover a *superpower*.

---

[73] Interestingly, all my course participants who spoke up nevertheless thought Hillary Clinton was the best candidate.

Summary

1. Pauses are OK.... they make you sound... smart.
2. Repetition is OK. So is repetition. Repeat your main message to help your audience remember it.
3. Deliver a great, winning and powerful message by using positive words!

Exercise

1. Watch a powerful speech by any of the people mentioned here or a popular TED talk. Ask yourself, do they use any of the advanced techniques mentioned here? If so, write them down.

2. What positive words can you associate with your speech? Write them down.

3. When you practice your talk out loud, make sure you speak slowly. If your mind goes blank, allow yourself two or three seconds of silence.

4. What are your main three points? Make sure you repeat them several times in your talk, using slightly different words each time. Hit that message home!

5. If you really want to study these techniques, watch a product launch by Steve Jobs, for example the iPhone launch. See how many techniques are used in this book. You will see many mentioned in this chapter (pauses, repetition and positive words). But you will also see *many* more: he is the *king* of the STAR moment!

I need to explain the main message of my presentation as clearly as possible. So here is the main message, summarised in just one or two sentences:

And here are the positive words I can associate with my speech:

Nice

"Doubt kills more dreams than failure ever will."
Suzy Kassem - poet, author, philosopher

Gradually I started to give workshops at larger, local business customers, like Philips, ASML and Eindhoven University of Technology. But one company completely took me by surprise.

In May 2018, a year into running my own business, I suddenly got a surprising LinkedIn invite from Amélie Laurent of the global travel IT company, Amadeus. She saw my TEDx talk and wondered if I would be interested in pitching to them to give an onsite Advanced Presentation skills workshop.

And not onsite at just any location: if successful I would travel to beautiful Nice in southern France.

They asked me for a written proposal. I had never written one for such a huge company before and spent a lot of time researching how to do it, to make the best proposal possible.

I submitted my best effort and waited. After a few weeks I heard back from them: I was through the first round!

Soon after they invited me for an online interview. I spoke with Amélie and two of her colleagues for over an hour. It seemed incredible: could I be chosen to work for such a huge and successful company?

My dream came true: they selected me to give a pilot workshop! So in October 2018, I flew to their wonderful, modern location for the first workshop. Even though it was mid-Autumn, it was beautiful, warm, sunny weather.

I remember being nervous again, just like before my TEDx talk. I was missing sleep and was getting more anxious about the workshop.

Would it be good enough for such a prestigious customer?

Despite my fears, the workshop was a big success. Now I give several workshops a year in Nice and I love it: Amadeus is a great company with very enthusiastic people and a fantastic location!

And it was on one of these very trips that this book was born...

99

Influence, persuasion, hypnosis: casting a spell over your audience

"I think the power of persuasion would be the greatest superpower of all time."
Jenny Mollen - actress

The power of the direct command

What is the very first word I used in my TEDx talk? I've already mentioned it earlier in this book - can you remember? When I ask this question during my workshop, I hear answers like, *"Hello"*, *"Welcome"* and *"Good morning"*. It wasn't any of these. These are all weak beginnings: they are dull and predictable and therefore not attention-grabbing.

The word I used was a direct command. From the very first word, I started to influence my audience. What word was it? I'll keep you in suspense for a while longer.

A few years ago I was at a conference for several hundred project leaders where I was running a workshop. As we entered the big conference hall at the start of the day, we were all given a cap. There were two colours of hat: orange and white.

Then the two guest presenters walked on stage. What happened next was a masterclass in persuasion! They looked at each other and said, *"That's strange, usually we get a huge round of applause when we walk on stage! Let's try again."* Then they walked off and walked back on again. Cue massive applause... the whole audience was already under their spell!

One of them put on his hat, the white one. He called out to the audience, *"Would those of you with a white cap please put it on? And now, if you are wearing a white hat, please stand up!"* 200 otherwise very serious technical project leaders rose to their feet. *"Let's give them a round of applause!"* And the whole audience applauded, even though the white cap people hadn't done anything worthy of applause.

Then the other took out his orange cap. He repeated essentially the same process with the orange cap. By this time every person in the room had both applauded and risen to their feet on command. Everyone except me.

Then the first one said, *"Everyone stand up! Give yourselves a huge round of applause!"* What do you think was going through my head?

I was thinking, *'If I don't stand up with the others, I will be the odd one out. What if they point to me and draw everyone's attention to me?'* But I remained seated. And the next thing that went through my head was, *'Wow, what power these guys have! We've never seen them before and yet they've got command over the entire room, including quite a few very senior managers!'*

And that's why I remained seated. I didn't want to fall under their spell, partly out of stubbornness and partly out of curiosity: what would it be like to *observe* this technique?

There are two lessons I want you to learn from this chapter. The first is:

1. Know the power of direct commands and don't let yourself fall under their spell if the speaker is using their power for a bad reason.

Can a speaker use these techniques to make good people do bad things? An experiment by a high school history teacher in 1967 showed just how easy it is. Ron Jones decided to show his students how easily ordinary Germans became part of the fascist Nazi movement. In a week-long experiment, he created a movement called *"The Third Wave"*. It started with rules and discipline. But when he got other students to enforce the rules, it quickly turned nasty.

I won't detail it further here; you can read about it on Wikipedia[74] or watch the 1981 TV dramatisation online[75]. You will have to get past the poor video quality (by today's standards). Caution: it is disturbing. Watching the true story

---

[74] https://en.wikipedia.org/wiki/The_Third_Wave_(experiment)
[75] https://youtu.be/ICng-KRxXJ8 *"The Wave"* (David McCarthy)

of how normal American students started to embrace parts of Nazism in just one week is scary and sobering. And a large part of his technique was simply giving his students direct commands.

What I want you to get from The Wave and this section is: be aware the power speakers have over you when you are in their audience. And direct commands can be so subtle: did you notice the previous sentence was a direct command?

So when a speaker starts to give the audience direct commands, take a moment to consider, *"Do I **want** to follow this command or am I just doing it because everyone else is? Do I want to be under their influence?"*

The second lesson is:

2. You can use direct commands.

Right now you may not feel comfortable using direct commands! However, direct commands can and should be used in your presentation: your call to action is a direct command. If you have good intentions, your audience will appreciate the clarity of your direct command. For example, in the project leader event story above, I presume the presenters had good intentions: they simply wanted to create a great, fun atmosphere (and they succeeded).

What direct commands can you use during your presentation, apart from the call to action? You can use subtle commands, like these:

- *"Listen!"*

- *"Write this down!"*
- *"Believe me!"* (A favourite of POTUS 45.)

These are all so subtle that, if you heard them in a speech, you probably wouldn't even notice that they were commands. But they *are* all commands and, as you start to obey them, you fall under the spell of the speaker. Their message becomes more persuasive. And when you learn to follow their easy commands (like, *"listen"*), you are more likely to follow their other commands, including their call to action.

My experience

This is why I was a bit reluctant to share this information so freely: I know how powerful this knowledge is. Call it what you like: influence, persuasion or hypnosis; I know it works!

At my workshop, I establish my authority right at the start of the day. I ask each participant to stand up and introduce themselves, giving one reason why we might want to contact them. And after that exercise I tell them that one of the reasons for starting with this is *influence*; I want to establish myself as the leader of the day.

As the day goes on, I notice that the influence that I have on the group grows. It might be in the obvious things, like whenever I give them a direct command, for example, *"Stand up and tell a story to the group"*, they do it without ever questioning it. Or it might be in a more subtle way: as I'm speaking I notice them all nodding at me... and the nodding increases throughout the day. Sometimes they even look like they are in a trance.

And if you think that is scary, what makes it more alarming is that these commands can be even more subtle than the command, *"listen"*.

The most subtle command

Do you remember that I told you earlier how to tell the difference between an untrained and a trained presenter? An untrained presenter will say, *"Hands up those who would like to use a call to action in their presentations."* That's a direct command.

The subtle version? *"Who would like to use a call to action in their presentations?"* As they say this, the presenter raises one hand and looks around at the audience. And they will raise their hands. The most subtle direct command is the one not spoken...

The John Lennon moment

Did I give any direct commands in my TEDx talk? As I said a few moments ago, in my workshops I often ask the group the same question I asked you at the start of this chapter, *"What was the very first word I used in my TEDx talk?"*

The answer is: *"Imagine."*

I said, *"Imagine it's Wednesday 28 August 1963."*

And there, in the very first word, is the first command. You may have heard the expression from the film Jerry Maguire, *"You had me at* 'Hello!' *"* Well, I had them at *"Imagine!"*

How to use commands to persuade your audience

It's very simple. Start with small commands:

- *"Who here...?"* a show of hands
- "Listen...", "Imagine...", "Believe me..."

and then build up further:

- *"Stand up."*
- *"Introduce yourself to the person next to you."*

until you reach your C2A:

- *"Buy this product today to get 10% off!"*
- *"Come and join our team!"*
- *"Fund this project!"*

Don't fear your nervousness in front of a group. Fear the great power you have over them!

With great power comes great responsibility

Do you see how *direct commands* can and should be used? As a force for good. They will help you to persuade your audience of your argument and to influence them to action.

And direct commands are necessary: your C2A (call to action) is by definition a direct command. That is the goal of your presentation: to make the world a better place by having people *do something positive*.

Let me state this as clearly as I can: this is powerful! Use this power for good.

And yes, each of those last two sentences was a direct command. So is the next one.

Be aware of the famous expression: *with great power comes great responsibility.* That's not just a warning. It's also a promise.

So watch out! If you speak too powerfully, you may end up Leader of the Free World[76].

Coming up...

Speaking of which, what about body language? How can you communicate your message not just verbally but with your hands? Coming up next: we will take a look at how a previous POTUS did exactly that, communicating in two ways simultaneously (verbally and with gestures). Prepare to be surprised at what you will learn from the master of body language.

Yes, that last sentence was also a direct command.

---

[76] *"In America, anyone can become president. That's one of the risks you take."* Adlai E. Stevenson Jr.

Summary

1. Only follow other speaker's direct commands if you *want to*.
2. You can and should use direct commands, but only use them for good!
3. Did you notice that both 1 & 2 are direct commands?

Exercise

You can train yourself to spot direct commands from speakers, even the subtle commands. The first step is that you need to be aware of this technique which you now are, having read this chapter.

The second step is: learn to spot the direct commands in this book. If you see one, highlight it or write it down. (Yes, that was one.) Here are a few examples from this book:

- *"Think about it!"*
- *"Take a moment to consider what you believe you cannot do."*
- *"Watch out!"*
- And the most famous one in this book: *"Imagine!"*

Then ask yourself: is your call to action a clear enough command? Is it direct? Write it down. And finally, write down other simple direct commands you can use in your presentation. Hint: *"imagine"* is an easy to use yet very powerful command.

Here are some simple, direct commands I can use in my presentation:

And here is my call to action, stated as clearly and boldly as possible. After my presentation, I want my audience to:

Becoming an author

"To Infinity and Beyond!"
Buzz Lightyear (Toy Story)

I'm normally very careful when I book appointments, especially business appointments. I check and double-check every detail and put numerous reminders into my online calendar. I *never* want to let down a customer.

Despite all this, there was one occasion when I made a mistake. Fortunately, it only affected me and not the customer, Amadeus. I had booked to travel to Nice for what I thought were two back-to-back workshops.

But a couple of weeks before I realised that we had agreed on only one workshop. Should I try to reschedule the flight and hotel? In the end that turned out to be more hassle than it was worth. So I decided to spend a day off in Nice.

However, I don't like wasting time. And so I had an idea. Several people had asked me if I could recommend a book on presentation

271

skills. The aforementioned Remco has a book[77], but that's in Dutch and many of my customers are English speaking.

So, on Wednesday 25 September 2019, I sat outside of my Nice hotel in the bright, morning sunshine. Equipped with just my laptop and a cup of coffee, I started to write this book.

Initially, I had the idea to make the *"story parts"* a work of fiction involving a guy who had to make a work presentation. And it turned out just as dull as it sounds. So I immediately junked those ten thousand words and instead decided to tell you *my* story.

That day in the south of France alternated between working at my laptop and, while it was charging, taking walks through the nearby forest. This turned out to be ideal for my creativity: an hour or so of dedicated writing followed by an hour of walking, thinking of fresh ideas and then back to the laptop.

---

[77] *Spreken met Impact* (Dutch for "Speaking with Impact") by Remco Claassen

And I must say, it *flowed*. I hardly ever experienced *"writer's block"*. On the contrary, I was writing about two things I knew well: my workshop (which by now was very well developed) and my life. For the first draft, I could hardly write fast enough.

Of course, it was still hard work. That first version took four months, writing every day. I often got up at 5:30 am to write before my family woke up. But even though nobody else saw a word in all that time, I was completely motivated. This book was in me and it had to come out.

That first draft was rough. But that was OK. That's one of the things I learned (again) from Scott Adams about writing a book[78]. And at the end of that, I had a structure; I knew what I wanted to say. I just had to write and rewrite while junking whole off-topic chapters and lots of poor attempts at British humour. In total, I've probably thrown away about 25000 words (equal to half this book) and rewritten almost every sentence at least once.

At the same time, I was working with my

---

[78] *"How to Write a Book"* - Scott Adams:
https://www.scottadamssays.com/2013/09/25/how-to-write-a-book

artist and my editor. And I was researching how to promote my book. And I had plenty of reviewers! I'm so pleased that I did not have to *ask* anyone to review it - everyone who reviewed this book for you kindly volunteered.

So now I've brought you up to date. Now you know my whole presentation skills story, from my childhood to now.

But what does the future hold? That's what we'll look at in the next story chapter.

99

Space, time and... body language?

Past & Future

When you think about the past, where is that in relation to your body? Which direction? When I ask a group this, do you know what they most often say? *"Behind me."*

And then I say, *"What about left and right? Which of those is the past?"* And here they almost always say, *"Left"*. Hence to the right is the future. I think this is because of the way we write, from left to right.

(Actually, I'm sure. On two occasions I've had people join my course from Iran, one of whom was Hani, the illustrator of this book. In Persian, they write from right to left. So they say that right is past and left is future. For a Persian audience, invert the advice here!)

What does this have to do with presentation skills? What you are about to learn will allow you to separate those people who have had great presentation skills training (or who have read this book) from those that haven't. From now on, you will see so many people (even professionals including media personalities) make the same simple mistake. But you'll get it right.

Using your hands to indicate time

Imagine that you are talking about company sales. You say, *"Sales are going up!"* and you indicate that by making a sweep with your left hand up and to your right: from bottom-left (past) to top-right (future).

Only for your audience that's not right. Picture what *they* are seeing as you stand in front of them. Because your left-to-right is their right-to-left. They're seeing your sales going back in time! They have to do extra mental processing to invert your message. And while they're doing this, they're not listening to you.

To avoid this, mirror your hand movement. So you sweep your right hand from the right up and to the left (bottom-right to top-left). *"Sales are going up!"* Now your audience gets it immediately.

Using your whole body to indicate time

How could you use body language to enhance these three lines from a speech?

1. *"Ladies and Gentlemen, when I started this company..."*
2. *"Today, the situation is..."*
3. *"In the coming two years..."*

You could stand on different parts of the stage (or front of the meeting room) to indicate and move freely between the different time periods. The three periods above are: past (*"when I started this company"*), present (*"today"*) and future (*"in the coming two years"*).

But remember: you need to mirror it! So, if you were giving this speech, where should you stand?

1. *"Ladies and Gentlemen, when I started this company..."* Stand on the *right (for you)* of the stage: the *past* for your audience.
2. *"Today, the situation is..."* Stand in the centre of the stage.
3. *"In the coming two years..."* Stand on the *left (for you)* of the stage: the *future* for your audience.

You can even stand in one time and point to others:

- *"Today it might seem strange to think that we started this whole company in my garage."* Stand in the middle of the stage (the present), pointing to your right (for your audience, the past).
- *"We need to start today to prepare for the business of tomorrow."* Stand in the middle of the stage (the present), pointing to your left (for your audience, the future).
- *"Next year we will look back on today as a turning point for our company!"* Stand on your left of the

stage (right for the audience), pointing to the centre.

Emphasis

"I shouldn't really tell you this, but..."

Almost nothing is guaranteed to get your audience's attention as much as these seven words! The combination of mystery and mischief is irresistible!

But how can your body language support this?

We've just looked at using the left-right axis on your stage to indicate time. What about forwards to backwards? That is, when should you be far away from your audience and when close up?

At the start, you will be further from your audience. You will use your catchy start, introduce the problem and hence focus on the *big theme* of your talk. Save your *"close-ups"* for when you need them: keep your powder dry!

Then, you can go for the extra emphasis: when you want to share a powerful lesson, a solution or a *"secret"*[79], walk a couple of steps forward and lower your voice. Your audience will now have two reasons to pay attention:

- you are coming closer to them, which is a little unsettling; just enough to raise their attention level
- by lowering your voice, they will have to strain to hear you.

So if you notice people giving you less attention, try this simple trick to increase the attention level. Because, if you don't have attention, you don't have anything: whatever you say is wasted if they're not listening!

This effect can be magnified if you have a lectern. For a speaker, a lectern is a place of security; it's your comfort zone. There is your laptop with all your slides. There are your notes, for if you forget your speech. And, most importantly, there is a place behind which you can hide the lower half of your body. If you're shy or nervous, this is a powerful temptation.

---

[79] Obviously not a real, confidentiality-breaking secret. But this is a bit of playfulness. Say something like *"I shouldn't really tell you this, but..."* followed by something borderline mischievous: *"...it looks like we're going to have another record year!"* If you can do that with a smile, your audience will love you.

But if you walk away from the lectern, what happens? Everyone's attention level goes up dramatically. Walk to the other side of the stage and make eye contact with the people there. Walk towards your audience for effect. Walk *among* your audience!

What about my hands?

"All you need is something to say, and a burning desire to say it... it doesn't matter where your hands are."
Lou Holtz - American football player, coach, and analyst

One question that occasionally pops up during my workshops is, *"What should I do with my hands?"* I think this comes from nerves because people don't usually worry about their hands until they appear in front of an audience.

So, what should you do?

The answer is: *forget them!* Just forget about your hands and let them do their thing. This is the best way for your hands to appear natural. And besides, if your presentation is great no one will even *notice* your hands unless you do something weird.

Speaking of which... a few months ago I was practicing a presentation in front of my wife. It went pretty well except for one piece of feedback she gave me: *"Can you please stop doing that thing with your hands?!"* It turned out I was wringing my hands nervously. Can you believe that? The guy who gave a TEDx talk on public speaking, gives workshops on presentation skills and even wrote this book was *nervous presenting in front of his own wife!* So take heart, we all get nervous. But I digress, it's a good idea to check (either with someone else or by videoing yourself) if you have any weird mannerisms, especially with your hands, before you present.

OK, I will digress just one more time: don't hold anything in your hands unless you really need it. Do you have slides? You may hold a pointer / presenter. Or you might hold a microphone.

You should also avoid holding your notes, especially if you are nervous. If you are nervous, people in the front row will see your shaking hands. If you are holding your notes, *everyone* in the room will see your fluttering papers.

What's the only thing worse? Holding a pen! For one, I'm incapable of holding a pen for more than two minutes without having ink dripping over my hands. And having your hands turn blue in front of your audience is a bad look for any presenter[80].

For another, and this is particularly for men, if you are holding a thick marker pen, the look can get quickly... awkward... especially if you hold it at waist height and nervously start moving it up and down. I won't elaborate further. If you don't understand, ask your parents.

Otherwise, forget your hands. At least, forget them until you need to draw with them...

Drawing with your hands

Occasionally at my workshop, people will ask, *"Is it OK to put my hands in my pockets?"* If you watched the Obama video[81] I recommended earlier, you may have seen what he did with his hands. He certainly forgot them for most of the time: they were in his pockets!

So my answer is, *"If Obama can do it, you can!"*

But when he did use his hands, he did something very special: he used his hands to *draw pictures*.

---

[80] How can it get worse? If I then develop an itchy nose... By the end of my presentation I look like a Smurf.
[81] https://youtu.be/5IDQDoxXHm0 *"Intern Q&A with the President (a West Wing Week Special Edition)"* (The Obama White House); first 2m13s

Now it's time for me to confess something. My plan when writing this part was:

1. rewatch the video and
2. write down three or four word pictures President Obama used.

But as I rewatched it, I was amazed. There were not just three or four word pictures: almost the entire two minutes are a masterclass in gestures.

If you didn't watch it, please watch it now and make a note of the body language that Obama uses.

How many pictures drawn in the air did you spot? I saw splashing through waves, an umbrella and a very special walk in the park, to name just three. I made a full list which you can read at the back of this book, in Appendix A.

Do I use gestures? Absolutely! I drew three times during my TEDx talk, did you see what they were? Answers in the footnote[82].

---

[82] A flag, a mug and a bridge.

And if you draw pictures in the air with your hands, you also draw them in the minds of your audience where they will stay for a long time. Now who needs PowerPoint?!

Coming up...

This book is not about giving *good* presentations. This book is about giving GREAT presentations. How can you ensure people will remember your presentation years later? That's coming up next as we go from Space to a STAR...

Summary

1. Use the left-right axis for past to future, but don't forget to mirror for your audience.
2. Use the front-back axis for emphasis.
3. Forget about your hands, except when drawing pictures.

Exercise

1. Watch another speech by Barack Obama online. A good choice is *"Fired up, ready to go."[83]* Make a note of all the drawings in the air he makes with his hands.

2. Ask yourself: do you talk about time during your speech? If so, write down how you plan to make use of the left-right axis to strengthen your message.

3. And are there parts of your speech that you need to emphasise? Write down when you can move closer to the audience.

4. Ask yourself: what can you draw in the air with your hands in your next presentation? Write these down as well.

---

[83] https://youtu.be/5AhRqg0ADbk *"Obama tells story of famed chant: Fired up, ready to go"* (CNN) filmed in 2016 or the earlier version from 2008: https://youtu.be/BjA2nUUsGxw *"Obama: "Fired Up? Ready To Go!""* (DNC War Room) Notice how Obama's use of his hands had changed over those eight years: he uses many more gestures in 2016.

Make sure you practice these parts of your speech. Note that your presentation screen must be off (or black) for these dramatic moments.

5. Then read and be inspired, fellow presenter, by this quote from that speech:

    "One voice can change a room! And if the voice can change a room, it can change a city. And if it can change a city, it can change a state. And if it can change a state, it can change a nation. And if it can change a nation, it can change the world."
    Barack Obama - POTUS 44

    Here are the images I've seen a practiced speaker (like Barack Obama) use:

    Here is when I talk about time in my speech and how I will use my body to communicate that:

    Here is when my speech needs extra emphasis and how I will use my body and tone to stress those points:

    Here are some simple images I can draw with my hands:

The future

"Prediction is very difficult, especially about the future."
Niels Bohr - physicist

So, what's next for Mark Robinson Training?

One thing I am sure of: I want to keep passing on the gift that I received, first from Remco and then from many other sources, the gift that I have developed over so many years.

I want to continue to help people from all walks of life: business people, technical staff, administrators, people who do voluntary or charity work or anyone who needs to speak in front of a group to give a 10 / 10, TEDx worthy speech.

But I don't just want to help them with their presentation skills. I want to leave the world a better place than how I found it.

So I also want to share more of the unique power of positive feedback that I learnt from Scott Adams and use on all my workshops:

- I want to help individuals like Daphne become better public speakers and present with confidence in front of a group.
- I want to continue leading teams to improve their presentation skills and to grow closer together: teambuilding.
- And I especially want to help more people like Hannah grow in confidence.

Who is Daphne? Who is Hannah?

You will meet them in our final *"story"* chapter, when I tell you about the power of positive feedback.

You see, I only allow positive feedback in my workshop. That's what sets it apart: the encouraging comments given by the group to each participant after their presentation. I am not only teaching them presentation skills; I am also teaching a far more important lesson. For me and many of my workshop participants, that lesson has turned out to be life-changing...

"

STAR moments

"You can't use up creativity. The more you use, the more you have."
Maya Angelou – poet

9 out of 10? Not good enough!

"I am easily satisfied with the very best."
Sir Winston Churchill - British Prime Minister

If you put all the principles mentioned so far into practice, you will easily deserve an 8 / 10 for your talk, maybe even an 8.5 or 9. You will have had a great start, kept your audience's attention the whole time, had a clear structure and a persuasive call to action. You will have amazed them with how well you present and can expect to be invited to give more presentations. People will compliment you on your presentations and that feels great!

But that's not enough. This book is based on my Powerful Presentations! workshop. So, we're shooting for 10 / 10; and no less. We want to create a talk that will make waves, that people will remember for years to come.

And that's why you need a STAR moment.

Think back to what you've learnt so far. You'll see that I often gave you a *template*; something you could easily copy, paste and adapt to your needs. You had templates for the:

- start (questions, intro and WII4ME)
- structure (problem, cause, possible solutions and recommended solution) and
- end (3MP + C2A + TQ)

You've even had a template to get applause!

But a STAR moment is not something I can give you as a template. I can only explain the ingredients, give you examples and then leave it up to your imagination.

Ingredients

What is a STAR moment?

- **S**omething
- **T**hey'll
- **A**lways
- **R**emember

The very best presentations have something in them that you will remember for years to come. That *something* will be **surprising** and of course **memorable**. Ideally, it will also challenge you to **think about the topic** in a new way.

If you've seen my TEDx talk, you'll know my STAR moment: the MLK start. It was:

- **surprising**: the last thing you'd expect is the anachronist effect of the *"I Have A Dream"* speech done with PowerPoint and
- **memorable**: the absurdity made it funny and therefore you are likely to remember it.

And it will make you

- **think about the topic** in a new way: if PowerPoint does *that* to such a powerful speech, what's it doing to *my* presentation? MLK could influence millions without PowerPoint, do we need it?

So now you've seen the ingredients, let's look at some examples. These range from easy to implement to something that requires a lot of planning.

Join the audience

I once gave a presentation where I started by talking about my family, telling my audience some funny and memorable moments we've had together. After about two minutes I stopped and said, *"If I were you right now..."* and at this point, I walked into the audience and turned to face the front as if I was watching my own presentation, *"... I'd be thinking, 'Why's he talking about his family? When is he going to start his presentation?' I will let you into a secret. My presentation has already begun! All will be revealed in a moment."* (By the way, telling your audience accurately what they are thinking is also a powerful persuasion trick.)

The point was that what I was saying about my family was directly related to the topic - I just hadn't told them how up to that point. Imagine the power of that for the audience: suddenly the speaker is standing *right next to them, part of them*. They may have thought, as I stood next to them, *"What's he going to do now?"* I could feel the rise in attention level. You don't get people yawning or even coughing when you do that!

What made it a STAR moment were those few seconds I spent away from the front and as part of the audience. Whenever someone leaves the front, the lectern or stage, people's attention always increases! They think, *'Where's he off to now?'* Attention especially increases if you approach the audience: people fear that you might pick on them to answer a question!

Two years after that, someone came to me and said, *"I remember that presentation you gave!"* STAR moments work!

The star vandal

One of the first times I gave my workshop, one participant made a simple, but unforgettable, STAR moment. In the afternoon of my workshop, I have the participants list the topics we have covered. Then I have each participant pick a topic to present back to the group, in their own words. This is:

1. to give them another opportunity to present
2. to learn by teaching and
3. to learn by hearing again from the others.

On one occasion I was in the *brand new* offices of my employer, TMC. Everything was new, including all the office furniture. One man had selected STAR moments as his topic to present back to the group. He took a big, thick *permanent* marker and said, *"A STAR moment means doing something your audience will always remember."* And then he took the permanent marker and drew a very large star on the desk in front of him!

I was *horrified!* I thought we'd never get that mark off the table! However, we did eventually manage to remove the star... but that will always stay in my memory.

The Rick trick

I once gave a workshop in which there was an amazingly powerful and yet super simple STAR moment.

Rick was going to give a presentation about a *company wiki* (a tool like Wikipedia but for in-company use).

He went to the front of the group, said, "Good afternoon", then turned around and walked through the door behind him, slamming it shut!

We all started laughing. He stayed outside the room for 5 seconds, then 10. After about 15 seconds, he walked back in and said simply,

"That's what happens if you don't have a company wiki: your knowledge walks out the door!"

All of us burst into applause and laughter, two or three of us even stood up! It was the shortest presentation I've ever seen in my workshop: 30 seconds, and he wasn't even in the room for half of it! And yet, it was one of the most powerful presentations, and one of the most memorable.

A great STAR moment can change *everything*!

Speak like TED to get ahead!

This first question is vital:
What was the *previous* section's title?

You may think, *"Why did he choose a rhyme?*
What's he doing this time?!"

The reason is quite elementary,
Rhyming words stay longer in the memory.
And messages that rhyme are made to
Enable the speaker to persuade you.

Take it from a marketing star,
Who used this to sell a chocolate bar:

"A Mars a day
helps you work, rest and play!"

Readers in the UK and Australia
Will recognise this slogan - it was no failure!

Used to sell Mars bars, you see
It includes a rhyme and the rule of three.

In the 90s a lawyer thought at one time,
He would summarise his argument in a rhyme.

O J Simpson was accused of a crime most chilling
Of his wife and her friend - their killing.

In front of the jury, he stood,
To make the best defence he could.

The question the lawyer had planned:
Was the glove too small for the hand?

And his lawyer won it, I admit,
By saying, *"If it doesn't fit, you must acquit!"*[84]

Rhymes stay in your memory, you remember the lines,
And are used to sell food, *"Beans means Heinz"*[85].

And rhyming is a habit that's hard to stop,
You could say, *"Once you pop, you can't stop!"*[86]

So use your speech as an occasion
For a little audience persuasion.

And take some extra preparation time,
To put your call to action into a memorable rhyme[87].

---

[84] Though O J Simpson was later found guilty in a civil case where no rhyming phrase was used.

[85] Slogan for *Heinz Baked Beans*.

[86] *Pringles* crisps slogan.

[87] For more on this, see *Pre-Suasion: A Revolutionary Way to Influence and Persuade*, Dr Robert Cialdini. And watch this short video: *The Rhyming Pitch - Revised* by Daniel Pink: https://vimeo.com/68960744 Rhymes are memorable and persuasive.

The long wait

A BAD presentation can seem to last a looooooong time. One of the most memorable STAR moments that I've witnessed made use of this. A man came on stage and said, *"We just need to wait a few moments... This presentation will start soon... Just a few more minutes, it will start, promise..."*

After a few more moments of either words like this or silently waiting he said, *"That's how our customers feel! They place an order with us and have to wait months for delivery!"*

Throwing away your notes

At the TEDx pitch event I attended, one of the other winners had a STAR moment. She started speaking with text on her slides and reading her notes, *boring!* Then she suddenly said, *"You know what, forget the notes!"* She threw them away in front of us and started speaking from the heart about her subject. The atmosphere went from dull to electric - we were hanging on every word as she suddenly started speaking with *passion*.

This moment was so good, I guessed it was staged. So some time later, I asked her if she had planned it. She hadn't. Perhaps the reason it was so powerful was that it was also authentic. She realised her delivery wasn't working and so changed it on the spot. That takes courage!

That was Kirsten Swensen who was another of the three winners that TEDx pitch evening. But Kirsten is not alone in this.

Partway through his *"I have a dream"* speech, Martin Luther King Jr's speech was not going so well. Mahalia Jackson, one of the singers standing close to Dr King called out, *"Tell 'em about the dream, Martin,"* referring to a speech he had previously given. He put aside his notes, told them about his dream... and wrote a moment in history.

Ilka's paper

During one of my workshops, Ilka went to the front to talk about STAR moments carrying a piece of paper. She started by saying, *"I've written out why STAR moments are so important."* And then she looked down at her notes as if she were about to read them.

I was horrified: Ilka was a great, natural presenter who seemed to *"get"* the presentation skills workshop and why this method of presenting worked. And yet, here she was, about to *read her notes to us!*

She later told me that she saw my expression at this point and knew she'd fooled me! Wonderful! So what did she do? She said, *"A real STAR moment is a moment that everyone remembers. It's not what you say but what you **do**..."*

As she said this, she ripped the paper into tiny pieces and threw them all up into the air! And she walked away to huge applause.

And then she walked back to pick up the paper because she didn't like to leave a mess!

Lists of 3s

"There are always three speeches, for every one you actually gave. The one you practiced, the one you gave, and the one you wish you gave."
Dale Carnegie - author & trainer

You may have already seen this in this book: whenever I have a list, for example in the *Summary* section of each chapter, there are very often exactly three items. Why is that?

First, I am not alone. Consider these examples:

- *"Veni, vidi, vici!"*[88]
- *"The Good, the Bad and the Ugly"*[89].
- *"Life, liberty, and the pursuit of happiness"*[90]

---

[88] Julius Caesar. It means, *"I came; I saw; I conquered!"* Each word begins with the same letter (alliteration, coming up in a moment). Since this phrase is 2000 years old, I think this illustrates both the power of alliteration and the power of three rather well!

[89] Six weeks after joining a new department, my boss once asked me to give a presentation. The topic? *"The good, the bad and the ugly"* of his department. That was a fun and powerful idea and gave me the opportunity to create a presentation that my colleagues remembered for years after.

[90] U.S. Declaration of Independence, 4 July 1776.

- *"... government of the people, by the people, for the people ..."*[91]
- *"We must pick ourselves up, dust ourselves off, and begin again the work of remaking America."*[92]

There are many more examples I could list. Three is a magic number in presentations. So make use of it: whenever you want to create a memorable list, try to make it a list of exactly three items.

And you can make that list even more memorable using an acronym or an alliteration...

The SEX guy: acronyms and alliterations

How many things people can remember from your talk? In the goals chapter, I said people will remember a maximum of three points. But a week, a month or especially a year later, even that number is optimistic with a standard presentation.

So with your 10 / 10 presentation, how will you ensure people remember those three points?

---

[91] POTUS 16, Abraham Lincoln, Gettysburg Address, 19 November 1863.
[92] President Barack Obama's Inauguration speech (lyrics from a song, *"Pick Yourself Up"*).

One way is to create an acronym: ensure the first letter of every word spells a new word. You don't have to use exactly three words every time (the STAR in *STAR moments* has four!) - but three is the most powerful.

Does it work? Well, do you remember the three possible states an audience will be in after a BAD presentation?[93]

I was asked to help a senior marketing manager prepare a presentation to over 300 software developers and managers. We agreed we wanted to make a memorable presentation that would result in action. We also agreed it would take a maximum of 10 minutes and would not involve PowerPoint.

The question was, how could we make it memorable? As we bounced ideas around, we settled on the three main points that the audience should remember:

- they should respond quickly to the customer,
- they could take advantage of the fact that they already had a great product that had better features than the competition but
- they needed to improve the user interface or the *"user experience"*.

---

[93] Bored, Asleep or Dead.

So, we hatched a plot and two weeks later the manager went on stage. As he spoke he started to write on a flip chart. At the top he wrote, *"WE NEED MORE:"*

He told his audience that they needed to respond faster to customer needs. As he did so, he wrote, *"Speed"* on the flip chart. Then he said that their USP (Unique Selling Point) was the unrivalled features of their product while writing, *"Exclusive".* Finally, he said that the user experience needed to be improved and he wrote, *"Xperience".*

People started to laugh but, in case anyone missed it, he drew a square around the first letters of each word: SEX.

Of course, this got much more attention than a standard PowerPoint presentation and was far more memorable. He is now known as *"The SEX guy".*

So use acronyms to make your main points memorable. But if you can't get your main points to fit a single memorable word (and you certainly shouldn't force it), an alliteration is a great alternative. Try to get your main points into three words beginning with the same letter. Do you remember the three Es?

- Education, Entertainment & Empowerment.

And what were the benefits of developing great presentation skills? The three Cs:

- Career, Confidence & Charisma.

What about the goal of your presentation? You need to hit all three Hs:

- Head, Heart & Hands.

Do you remember what 3Ps all stories need?

- A Person, a Problem and a Point.

Do you know what else is an alliteration? From this section's title: *"acronyms and alliterations!"*

Plastic bag

Still in the realm of fairly simple STAR moments is this example by a student. Though this happened two years ago, I still remember his presentation because of his STAR moment. This shows the power and necessity of including a *"Something They'll Always Remember"* moment.

His topic was about making affordable, sustainable housing from just a few simple ingredients. But the audience didn't know that when he walked on: they just saw a student... with a plastic carrier bag.

He put the bag onto a high table that was on the stage and then started his speech, at first ignoring his bag. It looked for a moment like he'd just come back from the local supermarket and suddenly realised it was his turn to speak!

Then he reached into his bag and took out one of the items which was one of the ingredients of a sustainable house.

Then he continued with all the items, explaining how easy they were to obtain, how they were sustainable, etc.

And he won the competition that evening!

What made it a STAR moment? We didn't know what was in the bag, so it was the *mystery* that kept us listening!

Drawings

A fairly easy way to create a STAR moment is to draw a picture on a flip chart. You're probably thinking, *'But I can't draw!'* I didn't think I could either.

Stop reading for 15 minutes and watch this excellent TEDx talk: Graham Shaw: *Why people believe they can't draw[94]*.

Done that? Now you can draw Einstein! And as Graham Shaw says, these simple pictures will help make your presentation memorable.

---

[94] https://www.ted.com/talks/
graham_shaw_why_people_believe_they_can_t_draw

What if you think, *"OK, I can draw simple things, but WHAT should I draw?"* Look no further than Noun Project[95]. Type in any term (e.g. *"teamwork"*) and get many great ideas.

So next time you have to give a presentation, take a moment to draw a quick illustration. You will need to practice this. Do this not only to get the drawing right but also the practical things, eg:

- Can the flip chart (and your drawing) be seen by everyone in the room?
- Do you have to hold a pen, a microphone and a laser pointer all at the same time?
- Is there enough paper on the flip chart and do I need a spare pen?
- Should I use one colour or multiple colours?
- Where will I store the pens when not in use?

Again - it pays to practice!

People will forget most of the words that you say. And they'll forget your slides. But that little drawing you do? That will be remembered for a long time to come.

---

[95] https://thenounproject.com

A live vote

In the Questions chapter, I told you about conducting a poll, by a show of hands, mainly to get attention. What about if you want a real poll? What if you want accurately to measure audience feedback?

Nowadays, that is very easy thanks to two inventions: the internet and mobile phones. You can easily set up an online poll via sites like Kahoot[96], Mentimeter[97] and others.

Using sites like these, you put a simple code up on the screen. Then you ask people to go to the site and type in the code. Your audience can actively participate and give you real-time feedback. You show questions on your screen and they answer via their phones. The results can be displayed in real-time for all to see.

These can be:

- **polling opinion**: *"My team would benefit from presentation skills training." Please choose:*
  - *Strongly disagree*
  - *Disagree*
  - *Neutral / no opinion*
  - *Agree*

---

[96] https://kahoot.com
[97] https://www.mentimeter.com

- o *Strongly agree*
- **a quiz**: great for testing the audience knowledge level
- **a word cloud**: ask the audience for feedback on a certain event or project in the form of single words; the result will be multiple words shown on the screen with the most common words **bigger** and the least common words smaller.
- **getting questions from the audience**: audience questions can be submitted by phone; you can opt either to have their questions immediately appear on the screen or have them only visible to you.

This requires preparation in advance: you need to get familiar with these tools, enter what you want your audience to see and test how it will look live.

The benefit of this STAR moment is that your audience becomes a part of your presentation: they are players, not spectators. Be careful though: you will need to use techniques like questions, stories, a video or maybe even another STAR moment to get people's attention from their phones and back to you. Better yet, give them a direct command: *"Please now put away your phones!"*

Bill Gates' TED talk

Now for the STAR moments that are harder to set up but have a huge impact. Again, these are examples of what is *possible* to inspire you to think creatively.

After Bill Gates left Microsoft, he put a lot of time and money into the worldwide battle against malaria. In 2009, he gave a TED talk on this topic. If you were him, how would *you* get people in America to identify with a widespread disease thousands of miles away, in Africa?

It's better to watch the STAR moment for yourself. It's 5 minutes in: Bill Gates: Mosquitos, malaria and Education (TED.com)[98].

If you don't have a chance to watch it right now, here is what happens. Gates says that malaria is transmitted by mosquitos. And then he picks up a jar containing live mosquitos and opens the lid...

He then says *"We'll let those roam around the auditorium a little bit."* And then says my favourite line in his whole speech: *"There's no reason only poor people should have the experience."*

Baam! The message is in the room: *"this could happen to me... this is happening right now to people just like me."*

---

[98] https://www.ted.com/talks/
bill_gates_mosquitos_malaria_and_education

Maths professor

Matthew Weathers is a maths professor. That doesn't sound like natural ground for a STAR moment, does it? But he has a STAR moment every year on the 1st of April.

My personal favourite is: *Math Professor Fixes Projector Screen (April Fools Prank)*[99]. Again, drop what you're doing and go watch that now.

In case you can't see it: he makes a permanent mark on his whiteboard and enlists the help of his clone, via a YouTube video, to help him out. OK, I can't explain it... just go watch it! :)

Weathers has a whole YouTube channel dedicated to these moments during his presentations. So if he can create a STAR moment for his maths lectures, you can create one for your business presentation. It will require you to think creatively. What can you do in your next presentation to make it *something they'll always remember*?

---

[99] https://youtu.be/Z9NQatne0xg *"Math Professor Fixes Projector Screen (April Fools Prank)"* (Matthew Weathers)

Coming up...

Now you know about STAR moments, you have a choice, as you do with all the techniques in this book: *use them* or *lose them*. Are you going to try out these new techniques? Will you dare to make a presentation that stands out?

That's the subject of our final chapter.

Summary

A STAR moment is:

1. **S**omething **T**hey'll **A**lways **R**emember.
2. It is surprising, memorable and will get them to think about the topic.
3. Examples include: walking into and joining the audience, a drawing or an object[100].
4. Lists of three: they are memorable, powerful and memorable.[101]

---

[100] How many times do I use the power of 3 in this summary? (Yes. Three times...)
[101] I said repetition is OK, remember? Now I've said that twice...

Exercise

Go somewhere you won't be disturbed for 15 minutes: take a walk or a shower. Think about your message, your goal and your call to action. What can you do in your presentation that people will remember for the rest of their lives? What will be your STAR moment?

Will it be a drawing or a prop (an object)? Will you do something dramatic, like walking into the audience or throwing away your notes? Will you use a list of three, an alliteration or an acronym?

Write down several ideas now. Then come back to them later today, tomorrow and the day after, adding new ideas, removing some and developing others. Eventually, your STAR moment will become crystal clear to you... and you will be ready to make an unforgettable presentation.

Here is a list of ideas or a mind map for possible STAR moments I can use for my talk. After writing these down, I'll pick two or three to think about some more. I'll imagine myself doing these STAR moments in front of a group.

Finally, I'll choose the one which works best (and gives me the most energy and confidence), I'll write down how I intend to use it here and then I'll practice it.

" The life-changing power of positive feedback

Success isn't just about what you accomplish in your life; it's about what you inspire others to do."

origin unknown

My USP

As I was preparing for my first workshop, I read a book called *"How to Fail at Almost Everything and Still Win Big"* by Scott Adams. He tells how he has tried many business ideas and failed at most of them! However, each time he *"fails"*, he learns a new skill which he can use in his next endeavour, skills like:

- business writing,
- networking and, of course,
- presentation skills

On the latter, there is a whole chapter devoted to his experience at a Dale Carnegie course on public speaking. I won't repeat it all here; I recommend you read the book.

However, there is one story he told which had a huge impact on my workshops.

The course Adams attended was made up of ten evening sessions. There were three rules for each evening (all of which I use in my workshop):

1. Everyone *must* present.
2. Participants choose when they present (no one says, *"Now it's your turn!"*).
3. Presenters get only *positive feedback*.

Adams tells the story of a very nervous woman who presented on the first evening. As she stood in front of the group, her sweat was dripping onto the floor. She was so nervous, she only managed a few words. Then she sat down, looking completely defeated.

Before I tell you what happened, ask yourself: if you were leading this course, what would *you* do at this moment? Before reading Adam's book, I would probably have said something like, *"Never mind, you can try again next week. Who's next?"* and tried to move on ASAP!

But the course leader did not do that. He simply said four words which enabled everyone to re-interpret what they had just seen. With those four words, he turned the woman's failure into a massive success.

He simply said, *"Wow, that was brave!"* And everyone knew what he said was true. She had given her absolute best and, while the results were not yet great, she had overcome a huge personal struggle to stand before the group and say those few words.

Adams said it was like he could see a light go on in her eyes: she was still in the fight. The following week she did slightly better and the instructor *praised her for her progress!* By the end of the course, *all of them* were capable of giving a confident presentation in front of their colleagues![102]

Positive feedback in practice

So how do I apply this positive feedback in my workshop? Each participant in my workshop gets a pad of Post-its. During a presentation, they write on their Post-its only what the presenter does *well* - no criticism.

---

[102] An earlier version of the story, written by Scott Adams, appeared on his blog: https://dilbertblog.typepad.com/the_dilbert_blog/2007/07/my-compliments-.html *"My Compliments to You"* (Scott Adams) And you can watch him retell the story in an interview: https://youtu.be/UPYiif7znZw?t=2450 *"SCOTT ADAMS: LOSERTHINK"* (Commonwealth Club)

At the end of their presentation, the presenter sits down (to applause, every time - that's also part of the *positive feedback*). Then the other participants take it in turns to read out what the presenter did well. Imagine that for a moment: you've just given a five-minute talk. At the end, your inner critic is already telling you what you should have done better. But then ten other people take the time to list all the things you did well. It's an amazingly positive experience. Finally, the other participants hand their Post-its to the now glowing presenter. This gives them a permanent reminder of their presentation achievements.

This approach of only giving positive feedback has often produced many surprising results. This is such an important, even life-changing, revelation, that I'd like to share a few stories with you. Then I'll tell you why it works and how you can apply it.

Positive feedback on the first-ever workshop

I knew this was going to work after the very first workshop with the TU/e (Eindhoven University of Technology) students, mentioned earlier.

They got into the spirit of it right away.

People *always* find positive things to say. During later workshops, I found that even when someone would just stand in front of a group and read loads of dull slides, the group would say, *"Wow, you really seem like an expert on this topic!"* There is *always* a compliment waiting for you to give - you've just got to search harder for it sometimes.

This positive feedback had a surprising effect on the students. They had never experienced anything like this. They told me that their university experience was the exact opposite. They were used to having their presentations *torn apart* by their audience, especially their professors. This was all in the name of learning, of course.

But what was the result of this barrage of criticism? At university, they began to *fear* giving presentations. A key component of a great presentation is self-confidence. However, they were learning the exact opposite: they were learning to be *insecure* in front of groups. And they were learning that message, the students told me, from their professors - who themselves often couldn't present well.

I knew this approach would increase their confidence and hence the quality of their presentations because that was Scott Adams' experience. What I didn't realise was the effect everyone giving each other only positive feedback would have on *the group*.

Bear in mind these students didn't know each other before the day started. But after a whole day of speaking words of *encouragement* to each other, it felt like they'd been friends for life!

The positive atmosphere was something you could *feel* - it was amazing! And I've felt it dozens of times since. If that positivity is all my workshops, and this book, bring into this world, then all my work would be worth it.

Hannah

At the start of some workshops, as people are arriving, I occasionally play music. One of my favourites is Madcon's *"Don't Worry About A Thing"* - not just a great tune but also encouraging lyrics to the nervous participants.

This was playing on one of my first workshops when Hannah, not her real name, walked in.

Hannah had been brought in by her friend, a colleague of mine. She had experienced a lot of tough times and rejection. And she had been unemployed for *years*. As a result, she was lacking a lot of self-confidence. My colleague had, perceptively, seen this workshop as an opportunity for Hannah to regain that lost self-belief. What happened tested both her *and me*. We were both about to have a life-changing experience!

The morning started in the usual way, alternating my theory with the participants' presentations. Then came Hannah's turn.

She went to the front and started speaking. For me, it was a good presentation. And she didn't use PowerPoint!

But then, two minutes in, she suddenly called out, *"I'm sorry, I can't do this!"* And then she ran out of the room.

I didn't know what to do. However, there were a lot of smart, caring people in the room. A couple of the women went off to find Hannah, who had gone to the ladies toilet. They spoke kindly to her and encouraged her to come back, which she did. (I found out later that they had advised her to do a Power Pose: see the chapter on self-confidence for why this works.)

I asked her if she wanted to try again or just watch the group. She understandably chose the latter. She watched as, one by one, the people around her each gave their presentations and *heard only what they had done well*. Throughout the afternoon, people were doing various exercises and still giving out positive feedback.

Finally, at the end of the day, they redid their presentations and all improved tremendously! This still gives me a kick every time! Then I asked Hannah, *"Would you like to have one more go?"*

She went to the front and delivered an amazing, confident presentation. I could hardly contain my emotions[103]. We all gave her a MASSIVE round of applause! I was so happy for her.

This had become a life-changing moment for her. She had faced up to and conquered a limiting belief, exposing it for the lie it was. She'd broken free of its chains!

The following week she emailed me. Here is an extract:

---

[103] I'm British. We contain emotions. We don't want them escaping all willy-nilly.

> *I want to thank you again for last Friday. I have such a good and powerful feeling about it. I haven't had that in years. You are incredibly strong in what you do. Good luck with your plans!*

My colleague, who had invited Hannah, sent me this message:

> *Hey Mark, just wanted to let you know that yesterday was a great and empowering day for me, but even more so for Hannah! Thank you for giving us this opportunity and I am convinced that Mark Robinson Training will be a huge success! You managed to create a safe space, entertain and at the same time give us professional, practical tips. Great job! Thanks again and see you Monday.*

Not long after this, I found out that Hannah had started working again. When writing this book, I contacted Hannah to get her approval for sharing this story and to confirm the facts. In her reply, she wrote, *"It was certainly the beginning of believing in myself again"*. Those words touched me. Experiences like this are, for me, the biggest reward of this work.

Would any of this have happened if we had given each other *"constructive criticism"*? Not a chance!

Daphne

Daphne[104] stood up to give her presentation, the last of the evening. All eyes were on her as she stood in front of us. She took her notes, which she laid on a desk near her. As she opened her mouth to speak, we all wondered - would any words come out?

To understand why we were all thinking this, I need to rewind this story a couple of hours.

We were gathered in a room at a Dutch university. My goal was to help a dozen students dramatically improve their presentation skills in just one evening.

The format was simple: each person would

---

[104] This section first appeared as an article I wrote on LinkedIn: *"The life-changing power of encouragement"*
https://www.linkedin.com/pulse/life-changing-power-encouragement-mark-robinson

present for five minutes and then the rest of us would give feedback. But there was one profound difference between this and all the other times when these students had received feedback. They were used to having their theses and presentations criticised - sometimes brutally so; that is normal for their level of education. They were used to having *"opportunities for improvement"* pointed out to them from a room full of peers and professors.

What they were not used to was **encouragement**.

And yet, that was the rule. Before opening the floor to the first presenter, I had made that clear.

"There is just one rule," I said. *"We're only allowed to offer positive feedback. Tell the speaker what they did well, not what went wrong. No criticisms or pointing out mistakes - just tell them their strengths. And make sure it is specific: not 'that was good' but tell them exactly what was good and why."*

I looked out at their skeptical faces. I'm used to this format, so I know it works. But nobody in the room did. So I added, *"Now I know you will think: how can we possibly learn if we only get praise? How will we know what to improve? Just watch what happens. And be prepared: feel how the atmosphere in the room changes."*

The first person got up to present; his topic, "Mexico". After he had finished, I invited the positive feedback. And so it came:

- "Great slides, your lovely pictures speak for themselves and it was good that you didn't use any text on the slides"
- "You clearly love the subject, your home country!"
- "You have a natural sense of humour when you present"

Then my feedback: *"It came across so naturally, did you practice out loud?"* He said that he had, a couple of times. *"It showed,"* I said.

The second speaker got up and delivered an equally interesting presentation, telling his story with a passion which touched us.

Then it came time for Daphne to speak. She went to the front clutching a couple of A4 sheets. To my surprise, she read the first sentence out loud to us, then the next and then... she kept on reading! She read her entire presentation!

I've never seen that before when coaching a group. This is a HUGE mistake in presenting - you lose eye contact, your speaking style often falls flat and as a result, you can easily lose your audience.

And yet... her content was very good. It was personal, with a story of how she was solving an everyday problem she - and a lot of us - encountered.

So at the end, we all gave our positive feedback. But I had a dilemma. How could I tell her not to read and yet keep to my discipline of only giving positive feedback? I couldn't. But I could ask her the obvious, honest question I had.

"Daphne, can you please tell me why you chose to read your presentation?"

She said, *"I was scared I would forget things. I don't feel comfortable improvising my text."*

She added that, as a seven-year-old child, she was taught to present by learning a pre-written text from memory. As she didn't have a lot of time to memorise this presentation, she had chosen to read it, word for word.

I suggested she think about it like a conversation: you don't need to get every word right, as long as you get your message across. Then I said, *"Daphne, this is a safe place. Would you like to try to present without reading it?"*

"Do you have any tips?" she asked.

"Well, there are two ways. One is you can write out your whole speech but with 10 keywords in a large font. Those 10 words are like your path through your speech, showing you the main topics to address. And you can always fall back on the full text if you get nervous.

"The second way, which I advise for this evening, is to take a blank piece of paper and only write down those 10 words. You know the topic well, those 10 keywords will be enough."

I asked her to prepare while we continued with the rest of the group, still only giving positive feedback, like:

- *"That was a great, personal story."*
- *"You are naturally enthusiastic!"*
- *"That's an inspiring message."*

With each speaker, the self-belief and mutual respect between everyone grew. The positive atmosphere, built on encouragement, was tangible.

Eventually, everyone had spoken and had learned from the feedback to themselves and to each other, while growing in self-confidence in presenting.

So I turned to Daphne. *"Would you like to try again now, without reading?"* She took her piece of paper with her 10 words on, went to the front of the group and turned to face us. She laid her notes on a desk near her. As she opened her mouth to speak, we all wondered - would any words come out?

She started speaking: one sentence, then two. Then she took a look at her notes to read the second keyword. After an "um" she continued, a few more sentences. Then she looked at the notes again, read the third keyword and continued, longer this time.

And after two minutes... she stopped looking at her notes altogether. She looked confidently at each of us, making eye contact as she told her story. But this time she told it with more passion, more humour and - surprisingly - even more content! Yes, despite not reading it, she found even more to talk about!

She finished speaking. The room erupted with applause. Not only had she presented well but we had just witnessed a minor miracle: Daphne would never need to read a presentation again. She now knew she could do it! She always had it within her; the encouragement from the group enabled her to release it.

As always, I closed the session asking what

people thought of the evening. Everyone mentioned several aspects that they liked. Some said they liked the tips on body language, or how to build up a storyline, or how to create slides. And every single person mentioned that they loved the positive feedback: the natural, specific encouragement. They found it interesting how you can learn just as much by receiving only encouragement, not criticism.

So here's my challenge to you: can you go one week with only encouraging your colleagues - no criticisms, not even the *"constructive"* kind? And if you could keep it up longer... what effect would that have on your colleagues? And how would that influence how they looked at you?

Daphne would never have been able to achieve what she did if we had offered criticism, even if it had been somewhat diluted with encouragement. What she needed was pure, raw encouragement.

And your colleagues need it too.

The team

About a year into my workshops, I was asked to give a workshop a whole team of people who worked closely together for the first time. What would be the impact of positive feedback on a *team*?

On the day, I got the usual great responses: the participants told me that they learnt a lot about presenting, grew in confidence and loved the positive feedback.

But what made all the difference was a message I got several months later. This showed me how encouragement can make a huge positive impact on a *team*.

I was conversing via WhatsApp with one of the participants and happened to mention the training day. She replied:

> Such a nice memory ☺

I was pleasantly surprised. So I asked her why she wrote that. Here is her response:

> That was one of the first sessions that we grew towards each other by giving feedback

> Positive feedback

> So thanks for making us aware of impact of positive feedback

Genuine positive feedback is powerful. So don't hold it back!

Let me say that even more strongly: if an encouragement comes to your mind and you don't speak it out, it's almost criminal.

But if you do speak it out, it can have a life-changing effect. It will cost you nothing: you can give it for free. It just requires a little courage to speak it out.

And yet the results of those few, positive words can change a person's life forever.

Me

Aside from business success, this positive outlook has had a far more profound effect on me. I have become a more positive person. Having spent the last three years looking for the best in people's presentations during my workshops, I've become less critical and less judgmental. And I've become more positive and more optimistic. I've also been more generous with encouragements. Doesn't the world need more of all of that?

A few months ago our family was at a restaurant. My seven year old daughter told me how friendly she thought one of the waitresses was - and how much she liked her hair! So I told my daughter to go and tell the waitress.

The waitress, a woman in her twenties, was having a busy evening but stopped when my daughter asked to speak to her. They were too far away for me to hear the conversation but I could see what happened. In those two minutes, she slowed down enough to hear and internalise the words of encouragement my daughter spoke: she heard praise for her friendliness (yes, and for her hair!). Her face lit up as she received the encouragement!

If you would like to become a more happy, positive and successful person, try my 5/95 idea: 5% criticism to 95% positive feedback. Or to put it another way, if you give someone criticism (and we're assuming it's constructive), don't give out any more criticism until you've said 19 positive things!

Why it works

Why does positive feedback work? Wouldn't it be better if I also told people attending my workshop what they are doing wrong? How can they improve if they don't get criticised?!

That last question is one that I hear often: it's so ingrained in our society: we believe being criticised is the best way to learn.

My experience, as related in this chapter, is the exact opposite. My participants learn best when I *only* give them positive feedback. But why is that? There are multiple reasons.

Confidence

People present best when they feel confident. When someone is nervous, they come across as unsure. To make a persuasive presentation, you must be sure of what you are saying and demonstrate that certainty in your words and body language.

When you hear only positive things, you start to believe that you *can* present well. And when you believe that you become more confident and so you present better. It's a virtuous circle!

But it's not only the words people hear at the *end* of their presentations. What do they see *during* their presentation? They see the rest of the group writing their positive feedback on Post-its.

Imagine for a moment what that would be like if the other workshop participants were also writing things the presenter was doing wrong. Then *every time* someone wrote something down, it would be a distraction. *"Oh no"*, they might think, *"What did they write down? What did I just do wrong?"*

With the *"only positive feedback"* rule, *every time* something is written, the presenter gets a little boost! *"Wow, someone else just wrote something! I'm doing something right!"*

Learn, by teaching others

Humans like to be consistent. That's a basic rule of persuasion[105]. So if a participant tells the presenter, *"You made great eye contact!"*, what are they telling themselves? *"I should make great eye contact in my presentation!"*

So every time they compliment someone else, they are teaching themselves. And by giving positive feedback dozens of times on the same day, they are ensuring that they remember what makes a great presentation and that they will put it into practice.

Faster learning

In my experience, when people are expecting criticism, they can become defensive. Rather than listening to the feedback, they are planning their rebuttal. But when they are expecting only positive feedback, their minds are open. They are willing to learn, and that

---

[105] *Influence: Science and Practice* by Dr Robert Cialdini.

makes learning faster.

And because of this, you can change other people's behaviour. I know this because someone used this exact technique on me, without me realising until long after the event. That someone was my wife!

We've divided the household chores between us. One of my tasks is emptying the dishwasher which I do first thing in the morning. Normally I do this every morning but occasionally... well, I'm too busy. And sometimes I'm too busy the next day, and the next, ...

On one of these occasions my wife used positive feedback to change this behaviour. Here I will pause to tell you she didn't realise she was using this technique until I pointed it out to her!

She simply said this: *"I really appreciate it when you empty the dishwasher in the morning."*

That was it; no trickery; just honest praise. What was my response? I thought to myself, *"I like that positive feedback, I like making my wife happy. I'll empty the dishwasher every morning without fail from now on!"*

By focusing on the *positive*, instead of criticising, her message was effective (my behaviour changed) and it was a pleasant moment for both of us!

They already get enough criticism

Even though the participants of my workshop only give each other positive feedback, they still get criticism. The world's worst critic is always in the room. Who is that?

Themselves.

I'm often amazed at how people talk themselves down after their own presentations (do you remember how I did exactly the same in the *"Speaking at TEDx"* chapter?).

They tell themselves off and give themselves brutal criticism, in a way they would never do to others.

But happily for them, the feedback does not end there. After they've presented, heard their internal critic and sat down, their fellow participants speak. They then hear all the things they did well. And that puts their performance back into perspective.

Life-changing

During the first two workshops, I asked

participants to summarise the day in one or two words. Here are a few of those quotes:

- *Empowering*
- *Positive*
- *Rediscovering Confidence*
- *Awesome*
- *Refreshing*
- *Liberating*
- *Out-of-the-box thinking*
- *Energising*
- *Inspiring*
- *Eye-opening*
- *Seriously Life-Changing*

Now you know the *power of positive feedback*. So you might ask, why would anyone ever teach a presentation skills workshop any other way?

No, I don't know either.

Don't believe me? Try it!

You may be skeptical. That's OK, so was I. Fortunately, there is a very easy way for you to discover the power of positive feedback for yourself.

For the next week, only give positive feedback, no criticism, to everyone you meet: your colleagues, your friends and your family.

And see for yourself what impact this has on the people around you, your relationships with them and on your soul.

To repeat the quote of one of my participants: it's *"seriously life-changing"*.

99

Life's walk of fame

"Hold on to your dreams. The future is built on dreams."
Peter Cullen - voice actor

Three things I've had on my bucket list are:

1. I've wanted to give a TEDx talk. Done.
2. I wanted to start my own successful business. Done.
3. And the third? You're holding it.

I believe we were all created to be unique. Whether or not you agree that we were *created*, we can all agree that we *are* unique. Like the *Hollywood Walk of Fame*, we will all leave our own, unique impression on this world. This impression is *by* us, but it's not *about* us. It's about the lives we changed.

The techniques in this book enable you to change lives for the better, if you use them.

Stand out

"You can't blend in when you were born to stand out"
R J Palacio - author (from the novel and film, "Wonder")

If you use them, you will need to dare to stand out, to break the mould, to be different in a world where so many presentations are so similar - and so forgettable. It will take courage, but the upside is huge: in addition to the Confidence, Career boost and Charisma mentioned at the start of this book, the *feeling* you get when you make a 10 / 10 presentation is amazing. All those hours of preparation will have been well worth it.

You *can* use them... or you can lose them. You can go into your box, stay in your lane, behave like your critics expect you to.

You've only got one life. So when you appear in front of the group or on stage, dare to give your very best and blow your audience away. Grab their attention from your first few words. Entertain them with powerful, personal stories. Use a STAR moment and get yourself, and your message, noticed. And give them a clear call to action: invite them to join you in making our world better.

Be brave

"The brave may not live forever, the cautious do not live at all."
Gina Wendkos (from the film, "The Princess Diaries")

It may not be obvious, but it is actually pretty scary for me to put my work out there in this book, for anyone to criticise. And yet I feel it is my duty to pass on this skill that I learnt. So I have chosen to speak: to inspire and empower you.

Now it's your turn.

If this book has benefited you, either by enabling you to give a powerful presentation, by inspiring you with my entrepreneurial story or by my message of positive feedback, then I have one last request for you, one final *call to action*.

Speak. Inspire. Empower.

"It is not the critic who counts; not the man who points out how the strong man stumbles, or where the doer of deeds could have done them better. The credit belongs to the man who is actually in the arena, whose face is marred by dust and sweat and blood; who strives valiantly; who errs, who comes short again and again, because there is no effort without error and shortcoming; but who does actually strive to do the deeds; who knows great enthusiasms, the great devotions; who spends himself in a worthy cause; who at the best knows, in the end, the triumph of high achievement, and who at the worst, if he fails, at least fails while daring greatly, so that his place shall never be with those cold and timid souls who neither know victory nor defeat."

Theodore Roosevelt - POTUS 26

Speak. Do not be afraid to speak. Speak out to share your knowledge and your ideas. Speak out what you've learned, including any lessons you've learnt from this book. Speak out your unique message in the way only you can. Let us all benefit from the knowledge you've built up. Life's too short to remain in the background: now is your time to come out on stage.

Inspire. As you become more confident through your public speaking, inspire confidence in others. Dare to share with them your vision of a better future. Encourage them to be a part of it. Inspire not only with your words but also with your actions. As your career surges, share your success by generously giving your time and resources to others.

Empower. As your charisma increases you will have greater influence: people will seek your approval. So freely accept others as they are, their authentic, true selves. Give them positive feedback whenever you have the opportunity - never hold it in.

Speak, to give the best of yourself. Inspire, to create the best possible future. Empower, so that others are the best version of themselves.

And especially speak out for, inspire and empower those who are struggling.

In so doing, you will leave this world better than how you found it.

That's *real* success.

Mark Robinson
Eindhoven
June 2020

Thanks

"If I have seen further it is by standing on the shoulders of Giants."
Sir Isaac Newton - mathematician, physicist, astronomer

Writing a book is an immense task. And writing a high-quality book which has practical value to the reader is too much for me alone - it requires a team. So I'm very grateful to the dozens of people who have given so much of their time to make this book a success.

First and foremost, thanks to my family. To my wife, **Annelies** and our **daughters** for their patience as I seemed to spend almost every waking moment for about nine months working on this book. Annelies has been with me the last 25 years of my journey and her expertise, encouragement and wisdom have made all the difference... my words are utterly insufficient to explain how much of a positive impact she has had on my life. And thanks to my whole family, especially **Mum** and **Dad**, for their ongoing love and support.

Thanks to my wonderful artist **Hani Javan Hemmat** for the great cartoons and cover and, even more importantly, the fantastic collaboration. Hani is not only very talented and creative; he's also a pleasure to work with.

Thanks also to my great and tough editor, **Simone Roach**. Simone helped me improve my sentences, corrected many errors and tried to reduce the number of exclamation marks! (See what I did there, Simone?)

Thanks to my reviewers: **Beena Arunraj, Trees van Domburg** (who reviewed two versions!), **Angelo Hulshout, Benjamin Jurg, Elpiniki Mylona, Dannie van Osch, Annelies Robinson, Esther Robinson** (Mum), **John Robinson** (Dad) and **Annabel Romijn**. I did not have to ask anyone to review my book - they all approached me to offer their feedback and gave huge amounts of their own free time to help make this book a success. Thanks also to the many people including my brother, **Simon Robinson**, for helping me to come up with the new book title.

Thanks also to **Erwin Hoogerwoord** and the entire **TEDxEindhoven team** for believing in my talk enough to enable all this to happen. And also thanks for the ongoing collaboration in my role as speaker coach.

Thanks to all those whose stories have directly impacted me and hence this book: **Scott Adams, Ilka Adriaans, Peter Boon, Pierre Brasseul, Loes Cortenbach** (approved references to TMC), **Natalia Fokina, Daniel Sastre García, Sandra Greven, Hannah, Daphne van Hoof, Anne Junge, Roxanne Kantelberg, Marc Keijsers, Zeynur Kerp, Riet Kooiman** (the French teacher), **Amélie Laurent** (thanks also for approving references to Amadeus), **Maarten De Leuw, Daphne Muller, Henk Niessing, Hans Odenthal** (approved reference to Sioux) **Marco Peters, Martin Rae, Serge van Rooij, Marco van de Sande, Daan van der Stek** (thanks for all the encouragements and wise advice, Daan!), **Kirsten Swensen, Callahan Tufts** and **Rick van Twillert**.

Some of those names listed above are from two incredibly entrepreneurial companies, TMC & ASML. In addition, I'd like to thank:

- from TMC, I could mention *so many* great colleagues but I will limit myself to three: my ever supportive Director, **Hans Schuren**, **Lotte Geertsen** who is always encouraging and the super enthusiastic **Lucie Orognen** who has arranged many workshops with me,
- from ASML, I could again name so many inspiring colleagues, but I will just highlight just two: **Jens Frielink**, who helped organise and record the auditorium talk and **Sander Hofman** who approved references to ASML.

TMC and ASML are two amazing companies full of smart, inspiring people. It's an honour to work for both.

Thank you especially to two inspirational giants who have had a huge impact on my life; without these two giving me some of their precious time, none of this would have been possible:

- **Thijs Manders**, founder of TMC. Thank you for creating a company which rewards and encourages entrepreneurial behaviour and for your personal encouragement to me, on multiple occasions.
- **Remco Claassen**, whose workshops have inspired me and thousands of others. You opened my eyes to the possibility that even a shy, nerdy guy like me can make a speech that has inspired many thousands of people. And if I can make that journey,

what I've called, *"from terrified to TEDx"*, then so can my readers.

Thanks also to two other groups of people:

- To **all the people who have so far attended my workshops**. With your questions, stories and imaginative presentations, you have helped make my workshop become what it is today. And many of you asked for a handout or a recommended book... it took a while but here it is!
- To **the huge numbers of people who have supported me in many other ways** during my time writing this book. Some of you have supported me online: you may never know how much impact a simple LinkedIn *"Like"* or a kind comment on one of my articles or on my TEDx video has had on me. And a huge number of you have directly supported my online book launch. You are all too many to mention but each time our paths have crossed I have been energised by your support. - thank you, thank you, thank you.

Finally thank you to **God** for, quite literally, everything.

Appendix A: Obama's body language

If you didn't watch the video I recommended earlier *"Intern Q&A with the President"[106]* , please watch it now. Then watch it a second time with the analysis below at hand. Notice how many things he *does* match exactly what he *says*.

The context: he is asked to comment on his *"relentless optimism"*. Let's compare his speech to his actions; what he *says* and what he *does*.

Now you may not agree with *every* bit of this analysis. But we can agree: Obama's use of body language here is a masterclass and probably way better than what you or I typically include in our presentations.

---

[106] https://youtu.be/5IDQDoxXHm0 *"Intern Q&A with the President (a West Wing Week Special Edition)"* (The Obama White House); first 2m13s

President Obama: what he...	
says	**does**
"Some of this is temperamental. People just have different temperaments. I tend to be a pretty happy guy."	Big smile, matching what he says about being a happy guy.
"I'm pretty sure this is because I was born in Hawaii. And, so I spent most of my early years in really pleasant weather all the time. Splashing in waves and things. That helped."	The way he walks up and down is very relaxed. At one point he even lightly kicks his right foot up into the air, as if kicking his way through the waves.
"As I get older, and certainly in this job, what helps me a lot is taking the long view on things."	The relaxed walk is replaced by a much more serious pacing, almost military style.
"I think so much pessimism and so much stress arises out of looking at things in this very narrow here and now"	He holds both hands in front, palms facing each other with a narrow gap between them.
"but the day to day sort of ups and downs and swings"	His right hand, palm down, is gesturing up and down.
"it's like the weather"	He gestures his right hand quickly from right to left like he is sweeping it away, demonstrating his point that the weather is temporary.
"you get an umbrella sometimes"	His right hand in a vertical clenched fist in front of him, like he is holding an umbrella.
"sometimes you take off your jacket"	Here is a very subtle gesture to imply removing something over him.

President Obama: what he...	
says	**does**
"but if you can keep your eye on the long view"	He holds his right hand out, palm down, gesturing to the horizon.
"not only does that relieve stress but it also allows you to make better decisions."	There is a very subtle gesture away from his body, as if the stress is leaving him.
"The things that last,"	He takes a step back, using the front-back axis, implying this is a more global point.
"the things that are important usually have to do with: How did you behave? How did you treat other people?"	He walks along in front of the audience, making sure people on the other side (further from the questioner) also get attention.
"Did you work as hard as you could have? Did you do your best?"	He gives a little shrug, implying he is asking a question of the audience without assuming an answer.
"The things you have control over."	Another little shrug.
"When I'm on my deathbed..."	Here is the three second pause, already mentioned earlier in this book. This long pause exactly matches this dramatic sentence. It's very powerful. He also gives a very small shake of the head, implying clearing his mind of distraction and focusing on what is important, exactly matching what he is speaking about.

President Obama: what he...	
says	**does**
"the things I will remember will be, you know, walking a four year old Malia to the park."	He holds his hand out *literally acting out walking while holding hands with Malia.* This is the clearest example of drawing with your hands in this whole video: it's a powerful moment, especially after he talks about his deathbed with his three second pause!
"I'm not going to remember some headline."	His right hand swings from left to right as if throwing something away, possibly a newspaper.
"I think that's helpful. But that's just me, it's mostly the Hawaii thing."	Another couple of little shrugs, matching his jokey end.

Appendix B: Hani's journey: "making it simple is not simple"

My name is Hani Javan-Hemmat. I am an engineer and as a professional hobby I make cartoons which are mostly published on my website Gilmard.com. I illustrated Mark's book: Speak, Inspire, Empower! It was an enjoyable experience that I would like to share with you.

Since the first day I started illustrating Mark's book, I saw it as a journey. It was challenging for two main reasons. Before I tell you the reasons, let me share something with you: I already attended Mark's workshop and I was familiar with the book's content. I knew that it would become an outstanding book about presenting. This raised the bar for making cartoons for such a book! Besides this, it was a personal challenge for me to make it simple based on my minimalist style. For each topic, I didn't stop thinking until I thought "this is the one!" I put some ideas on paper which weren't quite right, so they faded out but to make room for the "right one". In the following paragraphs, I'd like to share some of these moments with you. Here are my designs, in the order in which I created them.

The connector!

Among all these cartoons, this one played a special role! The professional relationship between Mark and I started

with this one. I made it for an internal company magazine to address the 'exploding slides' problem! Mark shared it on his network and it got a lot of reactions. Surprisingly, it was an issue almost everywhere. This perfectly matches what you find in Mark's book: don't make slides like this! If we remember this cartoon while making our slides, I am sure there will be lots of darlings to kill, several other aspects to consider (the 3 Es) and... you have read the book, you know what I mean.

Mark Robinson's Cartoon Character

I suggested to Mark to have his own character in some of the cartoons :-)

The character needed to be (1) in a minimalist, simple style, (2) consistent in all the cartoons, and (3) most importantly, similar enough to be recognised as its real life counterpart: Mark!

352

It was a nice challenge and of course, not easy. I tried to find the most important features of Mark's face, which can ensure whoever knows Mark can quickly recognise his cartoon character. After a few drafts, this character was finally born.

Terrified!

This is the first cartoon I made for Mark's book. It simply

 shows each of us chained in our limiting beliefs! The main feature is that we are chained, but still not giving up. The situation can be exhausting but we may need someone or something to release us.

The 3C Knight

The Knight is Mark's favourite character. This cartoon

portrays how this book promises to guide us through a quest from our initial, frustrated state towards a knight state, who is stepping up to the stage, while raising his

hand as a symbol of self-confidence just before a victory.

E3

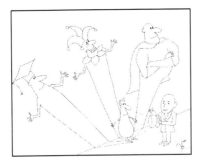

This is one of my favourites and shows how Mark highlights the three main sides of each presenter that should be on the stage with us to guarantee a victorious presentation.

The goal: H3

To ace the presentation, you need to aim at the right targets and at all of the targets. The corresponding chapter not only shows you these three

arrows as your toolset, but also helps you properly to aim them to ensure a hit!

Kill your darlings!

There is a funny fact about this cartoon: it was not made for this book. It was made even before the existence of this book. However, it is inspired by Mark's workshop. I know for sure that killing your darlings is not easy at all, because they are simply your darlings! But trust me as someone who did that, you won't regret it!

How to start!

Attending several presentations at work or university, this cartoon is the most tangible to me. This cartoon, as a mirror, just shows us how our presentation can become if some simple yet effective techniques are not applied. I don't like to attend such a presentation!

Structure is the key!

Sometimes having enough thoughts and ideas for a  presentation could be an issue for us. This can be solved by spending time in preparation. A more important issue is how to organise these ideas when we finally have them. This cartoon shows how Mark proposes several techniques to both trim and structure our ideas. These methods can be used even beyond presentations.

Launch them into action

As a knight of the 3Cs on the stage, you should be able to empower your audience to be launched! This cartoon shows how you can guide your audience to fly, while you have opened your powerful wings as a strong proof! As depicted, your audience are flying with  their own wings inspired by yours.

How to finish!

This cartoon existed after a few brainstorming sessions with Mark. He has had the experiences of both 'having a successful presentation' and 'finishing a marathon run'. So when he suggested "someone crossing the finish line on the stage" it wasn't an accident!

Power of questions

This cartoon illustrates how you own the minds and hearts of your audience by asking the right questions at the right time! I think you must have mastered that after reading this book.

Once upon a time...

As the cartoon shows, when you make the right story, it attracts your audience like a magnet. They pay all their attention to you and your story. This cartoon features three main elements: (1) you as the story teller on the stage, (2) your audience in a very relaxed and enjoyable pose, (3) and not distracted by all the electronic devices.

The elephant in the room

It may seem harsh at the first glance! Yes, this is intentional. This cartoon tries to show us how painful it could be for the

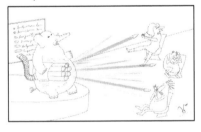

audience when we just shoot them with items and bullets. The point is that we may not be aware of the pain like the elephant with the closed eyes in the cartoon! Remembering this harsh cartoon can help us to think again whenever we are adding bullets after bullets in our presentation. Let's be kinder to our audience.

A treasure chest of extras

Mark suggested a treasure chest for this cartoon. But I felt

that didn't fit. I waited a significant amount of time to come up with this idea, but I think it was worth it! This set of techniques is like a Swiss Army knife. We can have it ready to use when preparing for a presentation. Each element is chosen to be as minimal as possible to remind you of an "extra treasure" that you can apply at just the right time.

Learning from the best

The famous knight of the 3Cs appears again as "the best" in

this cartoon. Having it on a poster on the wall indicates you don't necessarily need to meet them to learn from them. Another delicate feature is that the small girl is following the knight with a wooden sword. We may

need to play with a wooden sword to master the game which requires us to play with a heavy Valyrian steel sword!

Influence, persuasion, hypnosis

If you are a fan of Star Wars, then this Obi-Wan Kenobi costume must be easily recognisable for you. This was also Mark's suggestion, as a Star Wars fan. The cartoon aims at the Jedi-like power you can gain as a presenter to influence your audience. Just be careful with this power!

Time, space and body language

While we are on the stage, we can utilise that space as a coordination system to indicate time! Personally, I really like it. Although it wasn't the first time that I have heard about this, how Mark explains it in his book is marvellous. You just transform into a time indicator on the stage and with every step you do and wherever you go, the

appropriate message can be conveyed to your audience! As shown, just remember that everything should be mirrored on the stage to seem right for the audience.

STAR moments

If I am going to choose one of these cartoons as my favourite, this is the one. Many ideas came into my mind while considering this but none of them satisfied me. Finally I settled on this one which reflects my perception of a STAR

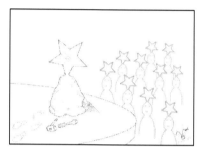

moment. There are a few elements in this cartoon . First is the STAR itself, which the presenter has made on the stage and it is sculptured also in the minds of the audience. It will be remembered forever. The abandoned spider web indicates the ages that come after this moment. Footsteps also emphasise this fact that the presenter is gone but the STAR remains. Finally, the closed eyes of the audience imply that they will remember this forever. Good luck with creating your own STAR moments.

Help! I am nervous!

"My fear is my friend!". After exposing my fears to the audience, they no longer scare me. They are mine, and this means I have control of them, can step over them, and even use them for my success. The famous Wonder Woman pose is also there to remind

you about the Power Pose technique mentioned in the book.

Summary and Exercise

 These two are to indicator the summary and exercise sections. I used Mark himself as the cartoon character because he did all these exercises in his  quest and now shares them with us. For the summary one, a delicate detail is that the summary is made by Mark and listed for us. The direction of the text is toward the reader. Also the magnifier emphasises how precisely it is done.

Branding logo!

 This is the last one I made for inside the book and I like it very much! As a simple and effective branding logo, this focuses on a few elements. (1) the three-tier title, (2) direction of each tier indicating the relationship between you and your audience (3) and there is a simple icon next to each tier emphasising its function.

Front and back covers

The front cover mainly focuses on the powerful three-tier title, where some cartoon characters are added to tell you the story of each tier. No more comment needed, it is designed to be self explanatory!

The back cover consists of three main elements. (1) Mark's hands as his sculptured signature on the book, (2) the red round TEDx stage (3) and the pose of Mark's hands empowering the audience and inviting them to launch!

Printed in Poland
by Amazon Fulfillment
Poland Sp. z o.o., Wrocław

60860601R00218